GENOA

TRAVEL GUIDE 2024 AND BEYOND

Explore Culture, Hidden Gems, Cuisine and Local Secrets on the Gulf of Genoa in the Ligurian Sea – Packed with Detailed Maps & Itinerary Planner

BY

JAMES W. PATRICK

TABLE OF CONTENTS

MY EXPERIENCE IN GENOA

The morning I arrived in Genoa, the city greeted me with the salty embrace of the Mediterranean breeze and the vibrant hum of its bustling port. This ancient maritime city, often overlooked in favor of its more glamorous Italian neighbors, possesses a charm that unravels itself slowly, like a well-kept secret. Strolling through the narrow, winding alleys of the historic center, known as the "caruggi," I felt transported back in time. The labyrinthine streets are a mosaic of stone, whispering tales of Genoa's storied past as a powerful maritime republic. Every corner turned presented a new discovery: a quaint piazza adorned with colorful facades, a hidden chapel, or a local artisan's shop.

The warmth of the Genovese people is as palpable as the city's history. On my first day, I found myself in a small, family-owned trattoria tucked away in a quiet alley. The owner, an elderly woman with a welcoming smile, insisted I try their specialty—trofie al pesto. As I savored the fresh, homemade pasta coated in a vibrant green pesto, I realized that Genoa's soul is best experienced through its cuisine. The pesto, a blend of basil, pine nuts, garlic, and Parmesan, was a revelation—each bite a symphony of flavors that spoke of tradition and love for local ingredients. One cannot speak of Genoa without mentioning its illustrious maritime heritage. The Galata Museo del Mare, the largest maritime museum in the Mediterranean, offered an immersive dive into the city's seafaring history. As I wandered through its exhibits, I felt the weight of centuries of exploration, trade, and adventure. Standing on the deck of a meticulously recreated 17th-century galley, I could almost hear the creak of the wooden planks and the distant call of the sailors. The museum's interactive displays and life-sized ship models make history come alive, engaging both the young and old alike.

The cityscape of Genoa is a striking contrast between the old and the new. From the bustling Porto Antico, revitalized by Renzo Piano's modern architectural touches, to the grandeur of the Palazzi dei Rolli, Renaissance-era palaces that are now UNESCO World Heritage sites, Genoa seamlessly blends the past with the present. The Palazzo Reale, with its opulent rooms and breathtaking frescoes, offers a glimpse into the lavish lifestyle of Genoa's aristocracy. The view from its terrace, overlooking the harbor, is nothing short of spectacular, especially as the sun sets and the city lights begin to twinkle. One of my most cherished experiences in Genoa was a visit to the Boccadasse district. This picturesque, former fishing village with its pastel-colored houses and pebbled beach is a serene escape from the city's hustle and bustle. Sitting on the shore, with the sound of the waves gently lapping against the rocks, I felt a deep sense of peace. It's a perfect spot for reflection, or simply to enjoy a gelato from one of the nearby cafes while watching the local fishermen mend their nets.

Genoa is also a city of hidden treasures. The Palazzo Rosso and Palazzo Bianco, part of the Strada Nuova Museums, house impressive art collections, including works by Caravaggio and Veronese. Yet, what struck me most was the tranquility of the museum courtyards, where one can sit and contemplate the beauty of the sculptures surrounded by lush greenery. The contrast of art and nature creates a serene ambiance, allowing for a moment of introspection amid the city's vibrant energy.

As I boarded my train to leave, I couldn't help but feel a pang of longing. Genoa had woven itself into the fabric of my travel memories, a city that had touched my heart with its authenticity and warmth. It's a place that beckons to be explored, not just seen. For those willing to look beyond the obvious and embrace the city's subtle charms, Genoa offers an unforgettable journey.

BENEFITS OF THIS GUIDE

Genoa offers a unique blend of old-world allure and modern vibrancy. This comprehensive guide aims to be your definitive resource for exploring this captivating city, providing you with all the essential information to make your visit unforgettable. Whether you're a history buff, a culinary enthusiast, or an adventure seeker, Genoa has something to offer for everyone.

Maps and Navigation

Navigating Genoa can be a delightful experience, given its well-preserved medieval center and picturesque coastal views. To make your journey smoother, detailed maps highlighting key attractions, transportation routes, and accommodation options are indispensable. These maps are available at tourist information centers, major hotels, and online platforms. Additionally, mobile apps like Google Maps and Citymapper are incredibly useful for real-time navigation and public transportation schedules.

Accommodation Options

Genoa boasts a wide range of accommodation options to suit every budget and preference. From luxury hotels offering stunning views of the Ligurian Sea to cozy bed and breakfasts nestled in the heart of the historic district, there's something for everyone. Notable luxury options include the Grand Hotel Savoia and Melia Genova, while budget travelers might consider hostels like OStellin Genova and Manena Hostel. For a more personalized experience, consider booking through Airbnb, where you can find unique stays that reflect the city's character.

Transportation

Getting around Genoa is convenient thanks to its comprehensive public transportation system. The AMT manages the city's buses, funiculars, and the metro, making it easy to reach various parts of the city. The Volabus provides a direct connection from the airport to the city center. For those who prefer to explore at their own pace, renting a bike or a scooter is a great option, especially given Genoa's narrow, winding streets. Taxis and ride-sharing services like Uber are also available, although they can be more expensive.

Top Attractions

Genoa is brimming with attractions that cater to diverse interests. The historic city center, a UNESCO World Heritage site, is a labyrinth of narrow alleys (caruggi) leading to stunning palaces and churches. Must-visit landmarks include the Cathedral of San Lorenzo, the Palazzo Ducale, and the iconic Lanterna, the city's ancient lighthouse. The Porto Antico (Old Port) area, revitalized by architect Renzo Piano, is home to the Aquarium of Genoa, one of the largest in Europe, and the Biosfera, a stunning glass sphere housing tropical plants and animals.

Practical Information and Travel Resources

Before you set off, it's essential to equip yourself with practical information to ensure a smooth trip. Currency in Genoa is the Euro (€), and ATMs are widely available. Most places accept credit cards, but it's advisable to carry some cash, especially in smaller establishments. English is not widely spoken, so learning a few basic Italian phrases can be helpful. Tourist information centers, located at major transport hubs and popular tourist spots, provide maps, brochures, and assistance in multiple languages.

Culinary Delights

Genoa's culinary scene is a feast for the senses. Renowned for its pesto, the city offers an array of dishes that highlight fresh, local ingredients. Don't miss trying trofie al pesto, a traditional pasta dish, or farinata, a savory chickpea pancake. Seafood lovers will delight in the array of fresh catches available at local trattorias. For dessert, indulge in pandolce, a sweet bread filled with raisins and candied fruit. The city's vibrant food markets, such as Mercato Orientale, are perfect for sampling local produce and delicacies.

Culture and Heritage

Genoa's rich cultural heritage is evident in its numerous museums, art galleries, and historic buildings. The city is home to the Strada Nuova Museums, including Palazzo Rosso, Palazzo Bianco, and Palazzo Tursi, which house impressive collections of art and historical artifacts. The Galata Maritime Museum offers insights into Genoa's maritime history, while the Museo di Sant'Agostino showcases medieval art. Throughout the year, Genoa hosts various cultural events and festivals, celebrating everything from music and film to food and literature.

Outdoor Activities and Adventures

For those who enjoy the outdoors, Genoa offers a wealth of activities. The nearby Ligurian Alps and Apennines provide excellent opportunities for hiking and mountain biking, with trails offering breathtaking views of the coastline. The city's parks, such as the Parco delle Mura and Villetta Di Negro, are perfect for leisurely strolls and picnics. Water enthusiasts can enjoy sailing, kayaking, and diving in the crystal-clear waters of the Ligurian Sea.

Shopping

Genoa's shopping scene is a delightful mix of traditional markets, high-end boutiques, and quirky shops. The historic center is dotted with artisan workshops where you can find unique souvenirs and handcrafted items. Via XX Settembre, the city's main shopping street, features an array of fashion boutiques, jewelry stores, and international brands. For a more local experience, visit Mercato del Carmine, where you can purchase fresh produce, cheeses, and other local specialties.

Day Trips and Excursions

Genoa's strategic location makes it an excellent base for exploring the surrounding region. The picturesque villages of the Cinque Terre are just a short train ride away and offer stunning coastal scenery and hiking trails. Portofino, a charming fishing village known for its pastel-colored houses and luxurious yachts, is another popular day trip destination. For history enthusiasts, a visit to the ancient Roman town of Albenga is highly recommended.

Entertainment and Nightlife

Genoa's nightlife is as diverse as its cultural offerings. The city comes alive after dark with a variety of entertainment options to suit all tastes. The historic center boasts a plethora of bars and pubs, ranging from cozy wine bars to lively music venues. The Porto Antico area offers a more modern vibe, with trendy bars and clubs overlooking the marina. For a taste of local culture, catch a performance at the Teatro Carlo Felice, the city's premier opera house.

CHAPTER 1
INTRODUCTION TO GENOA

1.1 Welcome to Genoa

Welcome to Genoa, where every cobblestone street tells a story woven into its ancient fabric. Genoa, often overshadowed by its more famous Italian counterparts, surprises visitors with its unique blend of old-world allure and modern vitality. As you wander through the narrow alleyways of the historic center, you'll find yourself transported back in time. The architecture here is a testament to Genoa's maritime glory days, with grand palaces and ornate churches lining the labyrinthine streets. The Cathedral of San Lorenzo, a masterpiece of Gothic and Romanesque styles, stands as a solemn guardian of the city's religious heritage. Nearby, the Palazzo Ducale offers a glimpse into the opulent lifestyle of Genoa's powerful ruling families.

Genoa is not merely a city frozen in time. Step into the pulsating heart of the Porto Antico, the old harbor area rejuvenated into a bustling hub of activity.

Here, the Aquarium of Genoa invites you to explore the mysteries of the sea, housing an impressive array of marine life within its modern confines. Adjacent to the aquarium, the Bigo panoramic lift provides a bird's-eye view of the harbor and the city beyond, a perfect vantage point to appreciate Genoa's unique blend of past and present. For those seeking culinary delights, Genoa's cuisine offers a tantalizing journey for the taste buds. Indulge in freshly caught seafood at the local trattorias or savor a slice of focaccia, a regional specialty that has captivated palates for centuries. The city's bustling markets, such as Mercato Orientale, overflow with vibrant produce and artisanal goods, offering a sensory feast for visitors eager to immerse themselves in Genoa's gastronomic traditions.

Beyond its architectural splendors and culinary treasures, Genoa enchants with its warm Mediterranean ambiance. The Ligurian coast, with its azure waters and rocky cliffs, beckons adventurers to explore its hidden coves and charming seaside villages. From the colorful houses of Boccadasse to the dramatic beauty of Camogli, each coastal gem offers a glimpse into the relaxed pace of life that defines this enchanting region. In every corner of Genoa, there is a story waiting to be discovered—a tale of explorers and traders, of artists and thinkers who shaped the course of history. The city's museums, such as the Galata Maritime Museum, delve into these narratives, celebrating Genoa's maritime prowess and its cultural contributions to the world.

As day gives way to night, Genoa reveals yet another facet of its allure. The vibrant nightlife scene, centered around the Piazza delle Erbe and the Piazza della Vittoria, pulses with energy as locals and visitors alike gather to enjoy aperitivos and lively conversation. From chic wine bars to traditional taverns, there's no shortage of venues where you can unwind and savor the essence of Genoese hospitality. Genoa is more than a destination; it's an invitation to delve into a world where history meets contemporary flair, where the sea whispers tales of distant lands, and where every moment is infused with the spirit of exploration. Whether you're drawn by its cultural heritage, culinary delights, or scenic beauty, Genoa promises an unforgettable journey that will leave a lasting impression on your heart and mind. Come, discover the magic of Genoa—where the past dances gracefully with the present, and each visit unveils a new chapter in this timeless story.

1.2 History and Culture

The origins of Genoa trace back to ancient times, emerging as a significant port city during the Roman Empire's reign. However, it was in the Middle Ages that Genoa flourished into a maritime powerhouse, establishing itself as a formidable Republic. This era not only saw the city expand its influence across the Mediterranean but also witnessed the birth of a unique Genoese identity—a blend of maritime prowess, mercantile spirit, and cultural diversity. The cultural landscape of Genoa is a testament to its storied past. The city's historic center, a maze of narrow alleys known as the "caruggi," preserves remnants of medieval architecture alongside Renaissance and Baroque influences. Here, ancient churches like the Cathedral of San Lorenzo stand as architectural marvels, adorned with intricate facades and ornate interiors that speak volumes of Genoa's religious and artistic heritage. Meanwhile, the Palazzi dei Rolli, a series of grand palaces constructed between the 16th and 17th centuries, reflect the city's affluent past and its role as a cultural hub during the Renaissance.

Art aficionados are drawn to Genoa's impressive array of museums and galleries, each offering a glimpse into different facets of the city's cultural tapestry. The Palazzo Bianco and Palazzo Rosso, part of the Strada Nuova Museums, house exquisite collections of European art, including masterpieces by Van Dyck, Veronese, and Caravaggio. These museums not only showcase Genoa's patronage of the arts but also highlight its enduring legacy as a center for intellectual and cultural exchange. Beyond its artistic prowess, Genoa's cultural identity is intricately linked with its culinary heritage. The city's cuisine is a celebration of fresh, locally sourced ingredients and centuries-old recipes passed down through generations. From the iconic pesto alla genovese—a basil, pine nut, and Parmesan sauce that epitomizes Genoa's culinary prowess—to its famous focaccia bread, every dish tells a story of tradition and a deep-seated love for gastronomy.

Genoa's cultural tapestry is also woven with threads of music and literature. The birthplace of Christopher Columbus, the city has inspired countless writers, poets, and musicians throughout history. The Teatro Carlo Felice, a majestic opera house dating back to the 19th century, continues to enchant audiences with its world-class performances and serves as a testament to Genoa's enduring passion for the arts. Visiting Genoa is akin to embarking on a journey through time—a journey that unveils layers of history, culture, and innovation at every turn. Whether wandering through its ancient streets, marveling at its architectural wonders, or indulging in its culinary delights, one cannot help but be captivated by the city's allure. Genoa's vibrant markets, where locals barter in the dialect of Ligurian, offer a glimpse into everyday life infused with tradition and community spirit.

As the sun sets over the Ligurian Sea and the city's skyline glows with a golden hue, one cannot help but reflect on Genoa's enduring legacy. It is a city that has weathered the tides of history, emerging stronger and more vibrant than ever. To experience Genoa is to immerse oneself in a living mosaic of culture and heritage—a tapestry woven with passion, resilience, and an unwavering spirit that continues to inspire travelers from around the world.

1.3 Overview of Neighborhoods

Genoa offers a unique glimpse into the soul of this coastal gem, revealing layers of charm and character that captivate and inspire. Let us embark on a journey through Genoa's most captivating districts, each promising a distinctive experience that will surely arouse your curiosity and beckon you to visit.

The Historic Center (Centro Storico)

Walking through the Historic Center of Genoa is like stepping back in time. This labyrinthine district, known as Centro Storico, is one of the largest medieval city centers in Europe. Here, narrow alleyways (known locally as "caruggi") weave through a maze of ancient buildings, leading to hidden squares and historical treasures. As you wander, you'll encounter stunning palaces such as Palazzo Ducale and Palazzo San Giorgio, each echoing tales of Genoa's glorious past. The heart of the neighborhood is marked by the majestic Cathedral of San Lorenzo, a testament to Gothic architecture that demands admiration. Amidst the history, the district pulses with contemporary life, with vibrant markets, artisan shops, and cozy cafes where you can savor the essence of Genovese culture.

Boccadasse

Perched along the eastern coastline of Genoa, Boccadasse is a picturesque fishing village that seems almost too charming to be real. This neighborhood offers a tranquil escape from the city's hustle, where pastel-colored houses line the shore and fishing boats bob gently in the harbor. The beauty of Boccadasse is best experienced by taking a leisurely stroll along the pebbled beach, feeling the sea breeze and listening to the soothing sound of waves. Small trattorias serve up fresh seafood, and gelaterias tempt with creamy delights, making it the perfect spot for a relaxing afternoon. The panoramic view from the cliffs above the village is simply breathtaking, offering a serene perspective of the Ligurian Sea that will leave you in awe.

Nervi: Further along the coast, Nervi is a neighborhood that seamlessly blends natural beauty with cultural richness. Famous for its scenic promenade,

Passeggiata Anita Garibaldi, Nervi stretches for over two kilometers along the rugged coastline, offering stunning views of the sea and dramatic cliffs. This is a place where you can breathe in the fresh air, take in the beauty of lush gardens like the Parks of Nervi, and explore art at the local galleries, including the Galleria d'Arte Moderna. The peaceful ambiance of Nervi, combined with its cultural offerings, creates an idyllic setting for a leisurely day spent amidst nature and art.

Castelletto

High above the city, Castelletto offers a vantage point that is nothing short of spectacular. This hillside neighborhood is known for its panoramic views of Genoa, which can be best appreciated from the Spianata di Castelletto. Here, you can gaze out over the terracotta rooftops, the bustling port, and the azure sea stretching into the horizon. The neighborhood itself is dotted with elegant villas, lush gardens, and quaint cafes where you can sip an espresso while soaking in the view. Castelletto's charm lies in its tranquility and the sense of escape it offers from the urban sprawl below. A ride on the historic funicular that connects Castelletto to the city center is an experience in itself, adding to the allure of this elevated retreat.

Pegli

To the west of Genoa lies Pegli, a neighborhood that combines maritime history with a leisurely seaside atmosphere. Known for its beautiful villas and lush parks, Pegli offers a glimpse into the opulent lifestyle of Genoa's past. Villa Pallavicini, with its stunning botanical garden and neoclassical architecture, is a highlight that should not be missed. The Maritime Museum, housed in the splendid Villa Doria, provides fascinating insights into Genoa's seafaring heritage. The beachfront promenade of Pegli is perfect for a relaxing walk, where you can enjoy the views of the sea and the distant silhouette of the city.

With its blend of history, culture, and natural beauty, Pegli presents a multifaceted experience that encapsulates the essence of Genoa.

1.4 Climate and Best Time to Visit

Genoa is framed by the Ligurian Sea to the south and the Apennine Mountains to the north, creating a stunning natural amphitheater. Its strategic coastal location has historically made Genoa one of Italy's most important ports. The city's terrain is characterized by steep, hilly landscapes that offer panoramic views of the sea and the bustling harbor below. Navigating Genoa can feel like a journey through layers of history and nature, as its streets weave between ancient fortifications, lush green spaces, and vibrant urban areas. The city is divided into several distinct districts, each with its own unique character and charm. The historic center, one of the largest in Europe, is a labyrinth of narrow alleys that open up to charming piazzas and hidden courtyards. The modern parts of the city, such as the business district around Piazza De Ferrari, seamlessly blend with the older areas, showcasing Genoa's ability to preserve its heritage while embracing modernity.

Climate of Genoa

Genoa enjoys a Mediterranean climate, characterized by mild winters and warm, dry summers. The city's coastal location moderates temperatures, making it a pleasant destination year-round. Understanding the seasonal weather patterns can help visitors plan the best time to explore this captivating city.

Spring (March to May)

Spring in Genoa is a season of renewal and mild temperatures. March can still be cool, with average temperatures ranging from 10°C (50°F) to 15°C (59°F), but by April and May, the weather becomes more inviting, with temperatures rising to 18°C (64°F) and occasionally reaching 20°C (68°F). Spring is an excellent time to visit, as the city is less crowded and the blooming flowers add a vibrant touch to the scenic landscapes. Outdoor activities such as strolling through the parks and hiking in the nearby hills are particularly enjoyable during this season.

Summer (June to August)

Summer in Genoa is warm and dry, with average temperatures ranging from 23°C (73°F) to 30°C (86°F). July and August are the hottest months, often accompanied by higher humidity. The coastal location ensures a refreshing sea breeze, making the heat more bearable. This is the peak tourist season, with many visitors flocking to the city's beaches and waterfront promenades. The lively atmosphere, coupled with numerous cultural festivals and events, makes summer a vibrant and exciting time to experience Genoa. However, it is advisable to book accommodations well in advance due to the high demand.

Autumn (September to November)

Autumn in Genoa brings cooler temperatures and a gradual decrease in tourist crowds. September still retains some summer warmth, with temperatures around 25°C (77°F), but by November, the temperatures drop to an average of 12°C (54°F). The fall foliage transforms the surrounding hills into a palette of reds and golds, creating a picturesque backdrop for exploring the city. Autumn is also harvest season, offering an opportunity to savor local delicacies and wines. The mild weather is perfect for leisurely walks through the historic center and along the scenic coastal paths.

Winter (December to February)

Winters in Genoa are mild compared to many other European cities. December temperatures average around 10°C (50°F), with January and February being the coldest months, yet rarely dropping below 6°C (43°F). Snow is a rarity, but occasional rain showers can be expected. Winter is a quieter time to visit, ideal for those who prefer a more relaxed pace and fewer tourists. The festive season in December adds a magical charm, with Christmas markets and lights illuminating the historic streets. It's a great time to explore indoor attractions such as museums and art galleries without the summer crowds.

Best Times to Visit Genoa

The best times to visit Genoa largely depend on the type of experience a traveler seeks. Spring and autumn offer the most comfortable weather for sightseeing and outdoor activities, with fewer tourists compared to the summer months. These seasons are ideal for those looking to explore the city's cultural and historical sites at a leisurely pace. Summer, while busier and hotter, is perfect for travelers who enjoy a lively atmosphere and are interested in participating in festivals and beach activities. The sea breeze makes the heat more tolerable, and the extended daylight hours provide ample time for exploration. Winter, although cooler, is suited for visitors who prefer a quieter environment and want to experience Genoa's charm during the festive season. The mild temperatures and occasional rain showers create a cozy, inviting atmosphere, perfect for enjoying the city's culinary delights and indoor attractions.

1.5 Local Customs and Etiquette

Genoa, a city steeped in history and charm, reveals its heart through the warmth and respect embedded in its greetings. When meeting someone for the first time, a firm handshake suffices. However, among friends and acquaintances, the customary greeting involves a kiss on both cheeks. This tradition, known as "il bacio," is a warm and familiar way of acknowledging one another. Picture this moment in the bustling Piazza De Ferrari, the city's central square, where locals meet under the shadow of the majestic fountain, their greetings echoing a sense of community and belonging.

The Art of Dining in Genoa

Dining etiquette in Genoa is a reflection of the city's rich culinary heritage. Meals are cherished social occasions, often extending for hours. When invited to a Genoese home, it is customary to bring a small gift, such as flowers or a bottle of wine. As you sit down to a feast of local delicacies in a cozy trattoria near the Porto Antico, you will notice the unspoken rules at play. Bread, for instance, should be broken by hand, not cut with a knife. The pace of the meal is leisurely, encouraging conversation and connection. Every dish, from the aromatic pesto alla Genovese to the savory farinata, is savored, embodying the Genoese love for food and fellowship.

The Evening Stroll (La Passeggiata)

The concept of "La Passeggiata," the evening stroll, is a cherished tradition in Genoa. As the sun sets, the city comes alive with people of all ages taking to the streets for a leisurely walk. This practice is more than just exercise; it is a social ritual that fosters a sense of community. Imagine joining the locals along the elegant Via XX Settembre, the main thoroughfare lined with shops and cafes, where the air is filled with laughter and animated conversations. This nightly promenade is an opportunity to reconnect with friends and family, to see and be seen, and to enjoy the simple pleasure of strolling through the historic streets.

Respect for Personal Space and Privacy

Respect for personal space and privacy is a deeply ingrained value among the Genoese. While the people are warm and welcoming, they also appreciate a certain level of discretion. In social settings, it is considered polite to maintain a respectful distance and to avoid overly intrusive questions. This cultural nuance is evident in the serene ambiance of places like the Villa Durazzo Pallavicini, a stunning historic park in the Pegli district. Here, amidst the lush greenery and tranquil lakes, you can observe how locals enjoy their personal space, engaging in quiet reflection or intimate conversations.

Deep-Rooted Religious Traditions

Religious customs are integral to the fabric of Genoese life, with the Catholic faith playing a significant role in daily activities and celebrations. The numerous churches scattered throughout the city, such as the grand Basilica della Santissima Annunziata del Vastato, serve as focal points for both worship and community gatherings. Attending a Sunday mass or participating in one of the many religious festivals, like the Festa della Madonna della Guardia, offers a profound insight into the spiritual devotion and communal spirit that define Genoa. These events are marked by processions, music, and shared meals, reflecting the deep bond between faith and community.

CHAPTER 2
ACCOMMODATION OPTIONS

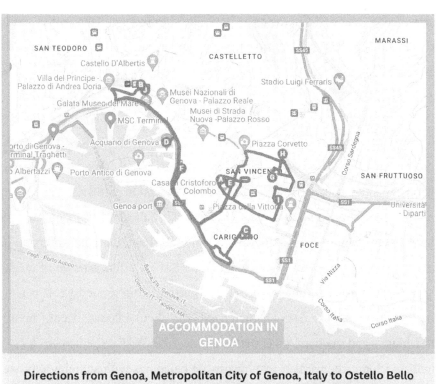

ACCOMMODATION IN GENOA

Directions from Genoa, Metropolitan City of Genoa, Italy to Ostello Bello Genova, Via Balbi, Genoa, Metropolitan City of Genoa, Italy

A	E	H
Genoa, Metropolitan City of Genoa, Italy	Hotel Bristol Palace, Via XX Settembre, Genoa, Metropolitan City of Genoa, Italy	Victoria House Hostel, Via Gropallo, Genoa, Metropolitan City of Genoa, Italy

B
Grand Hotel Savoia, Via Arsenale di Terra, Genoa, Metropolitan City of Genoa, Italy

C	F	I
Meliá, Via Corsica, Genoa, Metropolitan City of Genoa, Italy	Palazzo Cicala, Piazza San Lorenzo Genoa, Metropolitan City of Genoa, Italy	Albergo Astro, Via XX Settembre, Genoa, Metropolitan City of Genoa, Italy
D	**G**	**J**
Hotel NH Collection Genova Marina, Molo Ponte Calvi, Genoa, Metropolitan City of Genoa, Italy	Hotel Nologo, Viale Sauli, Genoa, Metropolitan City of Genoa, Italy	Ostello Bello Genova, Via Balbi, Genoa, Metropolitan City of Genoa, Italy

2.1 Luxury Hotels

Genoa offers a selection of luxury hotels that promise not only comfort and convenience but also a taste of the city's grandeur. This guide explores exceptional luxury accommodations in Genoa, highlighting their locations, amenities, unique features, special services, dining options, and how to book a stay.

Grand Hotel Savoia

Located in the heart of Genoa, the Grand Hotel Savoia is an iconic establishment that exudes elegance and sophistication. Situated near the main train station, Piazza Principe, and within walking distance of major attractions like the Aquarium of Genoa and the historic old town, the hotel offers an ideal base for exploring the city. The Grand Hotel Savoia offers a range of elegantly appointed rooms and suites, with prices starting from around €150 per night. The accommodations are characterized by their classic decor, luxurious furnishings, and modern amenities such as free Wi-Fi, flat-screen TVs, and minibars. Some rooms also feature private balconies with stunning city views. Dining at the Grand Hotel Savoia is an exquisite experience, with the in-house restaurant, Ristorante Salgari, serving a delightful mix of Ligurian and international cuisine. Meal prices vary, with a typical dinner costing around €50 per person. For reservations and more information, visitors can visit the hotel's official website (https://www.grandhotelsavoia.it).

Melia Genova

Melia Genova combines contemporary luxury with classic Italian charm. This five-star hotel is a short walk from the bustling Via XX Settembre and offers easy access to Genoa's main attractions, including the Palazzo Ducale and the vibrant port area. Melia Genova's rooms and suites are designed with modern elegance, featuring amenities like rainfall showers, Nespresso machines, and complimentary Wi-Fi. Prices for lodging begin at approximately €180 per night.

The hotel also offers The Level, an exclusive service providing personalized check-in, access to a private lounge, and enhanced room amenities. The hotel's signature restaurant, Blue Lounge & Restaurant, offers a refined dining experience with a menu that blends local and international flavors. Dining costs can vary, with an average meal priced at €45 per person. For bookings and additional information, prospective guests can visit: (https://www.melia.com).

Hotel Bristol Palace

Hotel Bristol Palace is a historic gem located on the elegant Via XX Settembre, one of Genoa's main shopping streets. This grand hotel, housed in a beautiful Art Nouveau building, is just a stone's throw from Piazza De Ferrari and the Carlo Felice Theatre. The hotel's rooms and suites are richly decorated, combining classic charm with modern comforts. Room rates start at around €160 per night. Each accommodation includes amenities such as satellite TV, minibars, and free Wi-Fi, with suites offering additional luxuries like Jacuzzis and separate living areas. Dining at Hotel Bristol Palace is a memorable experience at the Giotto Restaurant, which serves traditional Ligurian cuisine alongside international dishes. The restaurant's terrace is particularly popular during warmer months. Dining costs at Giotto average around €40 per person. For more details and to make a reservation, visitors can go to: (https://www.hotelbristolpalace.it).

NH Collection Genova Marina

Situated directly on the waterfront, NH Collection Genova Marina offers guests a unique maritime experience with stunning views of the marina and the Ligurian Sea. This contemporary hotel is part of the Porto Antico area, making it ideal for those wanting to explore the Aquarium of Genoa and the Galata Maritime Museum. The hotel's rooms are modern and stylish, featuring amenities like flat-screen TVs, coffee makers, and free Wi-Fi. Prices for accommodation start at approximately €140 per night. Many rooms boast private balconies with picturesque views of the marina. The in-house restaurant, Il Gozzo, specializes in fresh seafood and Italian cuisine, with an emphasis on local ingredients. Guests can expect to pay around €50 per person for a meal. For reservations and more details, visitors can check: (https://www.nh-hotels.com).

Palazzo Cicala

Palazzo Cicala is a boutique luxury hotel located in the heart of Genoa's historic center, near the San Lorenzo Cathedral. This charming hotel offers a blend of historical architecture and contemporary design, providing a unique and intimate experience for its guests. Accommodations at Palazzo Cicala range from standard rooms to spacious suites, with prices starting at about €130 per night. The rooms feature high ceilings, original frescoes, and modern amenities such as flat-screen TVs, minibars, and complimentary Wi-Fi. Unique features of Palazzo Cicala include its historical setting and personalized service. The hotel offers concierge services that can assist with arranging private tours, transportation, and other bespoke services to enhance the guest experience. For more information and to book a stay, visitors can visit: (https://www.palazzocicala.it).

2.2 Budget Hotels and Hostels

Genoa offers a variety of budget hotels and hostels that provide comfort, convenience, and a chance to experience the city's charm without breaking the bank. This guide delves into a variety of such establishments, highlighting their locations, lodging prices, amenities, unique features, special services, and dining options, ensuring visitors have all the necessary information for a memorable stay.

Hotel Nologo

Situated in the heart of Genoa, Hotel Nologo is a modern and trendy budget hotel that caters to both solo travelers and families. Located just a short walk from the Genova Brignole train station, it offers easy access to the city's main attractions. The lodging prices at Hotel Nologo start at approximately €60 per night for a standard double room, making it an affordable option for budget-conscious travelers. The hotel boasts an array of amenities, including free Wi-Fi, air conditioning, and a vibrant common area where guests can socialize. Unique to Hotel Nologo is its musical theme, with each floor dedicated to a different genre of music, creating a lively and engaging atmosphere. The hotel also provides a self-service breakfast area where guests can purchase breakfast items starting from €5. For those interested in exploring the city, Hotel Nologo offers bike rentals and provides useful information about local tours and activities. More details and reservations can be made through their official website: (https://www.hotelnologo.it).

Victoria House Hostel

Located in the bustling Piazza della Vittoria, Victoria House Hostel offers a cozy and social environment for travelers. This hostel is particularly popular among backpackers and young travelers due to its central location and budget-friendly rates, with dormitory beds starting at €25 per night. Victoria House Hostel features free Wi-Fi, a shared kitchen, and a common lounge area equipped with board games and a library. The hostel's unique feature is its rooftop terrace, which offers stunning views of the city and a perfect spot for evening relaxation. Guests can also enjoy complimentary breakfast and weekly social events, such as pizza nights and guided pub crawls. The hostel's staff is known for being friendly and helpful, offering personalized recommendations for sightseeing and dining. To book a stay at Victoria House Hostel, visitors can check their official website: (https://www.victoriahousehostel.com).

Albergo Astro

Albergo Astro, a family-run budget hotel, is nestled in the historic center of Genoa, close to Via XX Settembre and a variety of shops and restaurants. The hotel offers comfortable accommodations at reasonable rates, with prices starting around €50 per night for a single room. Guests at Albergo Astro can enjoy amenities such as free Wi-Fi, a 24-hour front desk, and daily housekeeping services. The hotel stands out for its warm, homely atmosphere and personalized service, with the owners often available to share local tips and stories. A modest breakfast is available for an additional €7, featuring a selection of pastries, coffee, and juices. Albergo Astro also offers discounted rates for extended stays, making it an ideal choice for visitors planning a longer trip to Genoa. For more information and reservations, their official website can be visited at:(https://www.albergoastro.it).

Ostello Bello Genoa

Ostello Bello Genoa, part of the renowned Ostello Bello hostel chain, is located near the vibrant Porto Antico area. Known for its stylish and eclectic decor, this hostel provides a welcoming atmosphere for travelers. Dormitory beds start at €30 per night, while private rooms are available for around €70 per night. The hostel offers a plethora of amenities, including free Wi-Fi, complimentary breakfast, and a fully equipped kitchen for guests to use. One of Ostello Bello's unique features is its lively bar and restaurant, which serves affordable meals starting at €8 and hosts regular live music events and social activities. Ostello Bello Genoa also provides a range of special services such as free walking tours, luggage storage, and even pet-friendly accommodations. The hostel's community-driven approach ensures that guests feel part of a larger family during their stay. Reservations can be made via their official website: (https://www.ostellobello.com/genoa).

Hotel Souvenir

Hotel Souvenir, located in the charming neighborhood of Boccadasse, offers a serene escape from the city's hustle and bustle while still being conveniently close to major attractions. This quaint budget hotel features rooms starting at €55 per night, with options for both solo travelers and families. The hotel provides amenities such as free Wi-Fi, air-conditioned rooms, and a lovely garden where guests can unwind. A standout feature of Hotel Souvenir is its focus on sustainability, with eco-friendly practices such as using solar panels and offering organic breakfast options at €6 per person. Guests can also enjoy the hotel's proximity to the beach and the picturesque Boccadasse village, known for its colorful houses and seafood restaurants. The friendly staff at Hotel Souvenir is always ready to assist with recommendations and bookings for local tours. More information and bookings can be found on their official website: (https://www.hotelsouvenir.it).

2.3 Boutique Hotels

Among the myriad of accommodations available in Genoa, boutique hotels stand out, providing a unique and personalized experience. These establishments are often characterized by their intimate atmosphere, distinctive design, and exceptional service. In this guide, we will explore various outstanding boutique hotels in Genoa, each offering a unique glimpse into the city's allure.

Hotel Palazzo Grillo

Located in the heart of Genoa's old town, Hotel Palazzo Grillo is a stunning 16th-century palace that has been meticulously restored to preserve its historical essence while offering modern comforts. Situated at Piazza delle Vigne, this hotel provides guests with easy access to major attractions such as the Genoa Cathedral and the Doge's Palace. Rooms at Hotel Palazzo Grillo are priced around €180 per night, offering a variety of options from classic rooms to luxurious suites. Each room is uniquely decorated, featuring original frescoes and antique furnishings that echo the building's rich history. Amenities include complimentary Wi-Fi, air conditioning, and a rooftop terrace with panoramic views of the city. The hotel serves a delightful breakfast with local Ligurian specialties, priced at approximately €20 per person. For more information and reservations, visitors can visit their official website (https://www.palazzogrillo.it).

Hotel Genova Liberty

Hotel Genova Liberty is a refined boutique hotel located on Via XX Settembre, one of the city's main shopping streets. This hotel occupies a beautifully restored 19th-century building and combines classical architecture with contemporary design elements, creating a sophisticated and welcoming ambiance. The rooms, starting at €150 per night, are elegantly furnished with modern amenities such as flat-screen TVs, minibars, and luxurious linens. The hotel also offers a variety of services, including a 24-hour front desk, concierge services, and a cozy lounge area where guests can relax after a day of exploring the city. Guests can enjoy a continental breakfast each morning, included in the room rate, featuring fresh pastries, fruits, and local cheeses. The official website for bookings and more details is (https://www.hotelgenovale.it).

Meliá Genova

Meliá Genova is a luxury boutique hotel that epitomizes style and sophistication. This five-star hotel is a short walk from attractions like the Luigi Ferraris Stadium and the scenic Belvedere Montaldo. Room rates at Meliá Genova start at €200 per night, with a range of deluxe rooms and suites that offer plush bedding, marble bathrooms, and stunning city views. The hotel boasts an array of amenities, including a full-service spa, an indoor pool, and a well-equipped fitness center. Additionally, the on-site Blue Lounge & Restaurant serves gourmet Italian cuisine, with meal prices averaging €30-€50 per person. Meliá Genova is renowned for its impeccable service, including personalized concierge assistance and valet parking. For reservations and further information, the hotel's official website is (https://www.melia.com).

Hotel Le Nuvole Residenza d'Epoca

Hotel Le Nuvole Residenza d'Epoca is a charming boutique hotel located in the historic district of Genoa, near the famous Strada Nuova. This hotel, housed in a 16th-century building, features original architectural elements blended seamlessly with modern comforts. Accommodations at Hotel Le Nuvole start at €160 per night. The rooms are tastefully decorated with contemporary furnishings and art pieces, providing a unique and artistic environment. Guests can enjoy amenities such as free Wi-Fi, air conditioning, and access to a common lounge area adorned with period furniture. A continental breakfast is served daily, with options including freshly baked goods, meats, and cheeses, costing around €15 per person. For more details and reservations, visitors can explore their official website (https://www.lenuvole.genova.it).

Grand Hotel Savoia

The Grand Hotel Savoia, located on Via Arsenale di Terra, is a historic luxury boutique hotel that has been welcoming guests since 1897. Situated close to the Genoa Piazza Principe railway station, it offers convenient access to both the city's historical sites and modern attractions. Rooms at the Grand Hotel Savoia are priced from €220 per night, with lavishly appointed interiors that feature elegant decor and state-of-the-art amenities. The hotel offers a wide range of facilities, including a wellness center with a sauna and hot tub, a rooftop terrace with a bar, and a children's play area. The on-site Ristorante Salgari offers exquisite Italian and Mediterranean cuisine, with meals typically costing between €40-€70 per person. The hotel is also known for its exceptional service, including a concierge desk, valet parking, and event planning services. For more information and bookings, the official website is (https://www.grandhotelsavoia.it).

2.4 Vacation Rentals and Apartments

This guide explores unique vacation rentals and apartments in Genoa, detailing their locations, amenities, unique features, and other essential information to help visitors make an informed choice for their stay.

Casa Acquario Oceano

Casa Acquario Oceano is a stylish and modern apartment situated in the heart of Genoa's bustling Porto Antico area, just a short walk from the famous Aquarium of Genoa and the Galata Maritime Museum. This location offers a vibrant atmosphere with easy access to some of the city's top attractions. The apartment features a spacious layout with contemporary decor, offering two bedrooms, a fully equipped kitchen, a living room, and a bathroom. Prices for lodging start at around €120 per night, making it an affordable option for families or small groups. Amenities include free Wi-Fi, air conditioning, a flat-screen TV, and a washing machine. One of the unique features of Casa Acquario Oceano is its large terrace with panoramic views of the marina and the sea, providing a perfect spot for relaxing after a day of exploration. The apartment is self-catering, but its central location means guests are just steps away from numerous restaurants and cafes, catering to all culinary preferences. For bookings and more information, visitors can go to the official website: (https://www.casaacquariooceano.com).

La Casa del Mercante

La Casa del Mercante offers a charming retreat in a meticulously restored 16th-century building. This vacation rental is ideally located near the Piazza de Ferrari and the Teatro Carlo Felice, providing easy access to cultural landmarks and shopping districts. La Casa del Mercante features three elegantly furnished bedrooms, a fully equipped kitchen, a spacious living area, and two bathrooms. The cost of lodging starts at approximately €150 per night. The apartment is equipped with modern amenities such as free Wi-Fi, a dishwasher, and a coffee machine, ensuring a comfortable stay for guests. A unique aspect of this rental is its historical significance and the blend of antique and contemporary design elements. The original frescoes and exposed wooden beams add a touch of authenticity and charm. Additionally, the apartment offers personalized services such as airport transfers and guided tours upon request. Guests can prepare their meals in the well-appointed kitchen or explore the local dining scene, with several excellent restaurants nearby. For reservations and more details, visitors can visit the official website: (https://www.lacasadelmercantegenova.com).

Genova Luxury Loft

Located in the trendy neighborhood of Castelletto, Genova Luxury Loft is a chic and sophisticated apartment offering breathtaking views of the city and the harbor. This rental is perfect for travelers looking for a stylish and contemporary living space with a touch of luxury. The loft features an open-plan design with high ceilings, large windows, and modern furnishings. It includes one bedroom, a fully equipped kitchen, a living area, and a bathroom. Prices for lodging start at around €130 per night. Amenities include free Wi-Fi, air conditioning, a flat-screen TV, and a washing machine. One of the standout features of Genova Luxury Loft is its private terrace, which offers panoramic views of Genoa's skyline, making it an ideal spot for morning coffee or evening relaxation. The apartment is also pet-friendly, allowing guests to bring their furry companions along. The loft is self-catering, with a modern kitchen that includes all necessary appliances for meal preparation. For those who prefer dining out, the Castelletto area offers a variety of restaurants and cafes. For bookings and more information, visitors can check the official website: (https://www.genovaluxuryloft.com).

Palazzo Penco Luxury Apartments

Palazzo Penco Luxury Apartments are located in a beautifully restored historic building in Genoa's city center, near the iconic Via Garibaldi and the Strada Nuova museums. This prime location provides easy access to many of the city's historical and cultural sites. The apartments vary in size, offering one to three bedrooms, with prices starting at approximately €160 per night. Each unit is elegantly furnished, featuring a blend of modern and classical decor. Amenities include free Wi-Fi, air conditioning, flat-screen TVs, and fully equipped kitchens. What sets Palazzo Penco apart is the luxurious ambiance and attention to detail in each apartment. High ceilings, original frescoes, and antique furnishings create a sophisticated and comfortable environment. Additionally, the property offers concierge services, ensuring that guests have everything they need for a pleasant stay. Guests can either cook their meals in the well-appointed kitchens or explore the numerous dining options in the vicinity. For more information and to book a stay, visitors can go to the official website: (https://www.palazzopenco.com).

Residenza Spinola

Residenza Spinola is a charming and elegant apartment located in the heart of Genoa's historic district, close to the Piazza San Matteo and the Palazzo Ducale. This location provides a serene and picturesque setting, perfect for exploring the city's rich history. The apartment features two bedrooms, a fully equipped kitchen, a living room, and a bathroom, with prices starting at around €140 per night. Amenities include free Wi-Fi, air conditioning, a flat-screen TV, and a washing machine. One of the unique features of Residenza Spinola is its historical architecture, combined with modern comforts. The apartment is housed in a beautifully restored building with period details such as high ceilings and large windows, offering a glimpse into Genoa's past. Residenza Spinola is self-catering, allowing guests to prepare their meals in the well-equipped kitchen. However, the central location also means that numerous dining options are available within walking distance. For bookings and more information, visitors can visit the official website: (https://www.residenzaspinola.com).

2.5 Unique Stays: Historical Homes and B&Bs

Genoa offers travelers a unique opportunity to experience its heritage through distinctive accommodations. Among these, historical homes and bed-and-breakfasts (B&Bs) stand out, providing an immersive glimpse into Genoa's past while ensuring a comfortable and memorable stay. This guide delves into remarkable properties, highlighting their locations, lodging prices, amenities, unique features, special services, and dining options, guiding visitors to make informed choices for an exceptional visit.

Palazzo Cicala

Palazzo Cicala offers an elegant blend of Renaissance charm and modern comfort. Located near the iconic Piazza San Matteo, this historical residence dates back to the 16th century, featuring beautifully preserved architecture and frescoed ceilings. The lodging prices at Palazzo Cicala start at approximately €120 per night for a standard double room, reflecting its luxurious yet authentic ambiance. Guests at Palazzo Cicala can enjoy amenities such as free Wi-Fi, air conditioning, and a daily continental breakfast included in the room rate. Unique features of this property include its spacious suites adorned with antique furnishings and artworks, providing a genuine sense of Genoese heritage. The hotel also offers concierge services to assist with local tours and reservations. The central location allows easy access to major attractions, including the Genoa Cathedral and the Old Port. For more information and reservations, visitors can access the official website: (https://www.palazzocicala.it).

Il Borgo di Genova B&B

Il Borgo di Genova B&B, located in the charming Brignole district, offers a cozy and intimate retreat for travelers. This family-run B&B is known for its warm hospitality and personalized service. Lodging prices start at around €80 per night for a double room, making it an affordable yet charming option. The B&B features amenities such as complimentary Wi-Fi, air-conditioned rooms, and a delightful homemade breakfast served each morning, with a variety of local delicacies included in the price. A unique aspect of Il Borgo di Genova is its beautifully decorated rooms, each with its own distinct character and antique touches, reflecting the city's rich history. The owners are renowned for their friendly demeanor and are always eager to provide recommendations and insights into local attractions and dining spots. To learn more and book a stay, the official website is: (https://www.ilborgodigenova.it).

B&B Al Centro di Genova

B&B Al Centro di Genova is ideally situated near Genoa's main railway station, offering convenient access to the city's key attractions. This charming bed-and-breakfast features rooms priced from €75 per night, offering great value for its prime location. The B&B provides guests with modern amenities, including free Wi-Fi, flat-screen TVs, and a hearty breakfast each morning featuring regional specialties. What sets B&B Al Centro di Genova apart is its commitment to providing a homely and welcoming atmosphere, with tastefully decorated interiors that blend contemporary and traditional elements. Guests can take advantage of the B&B's proximity to popular sites like the Royal Palace and the vibrant Via Garibaldi. The staff is always available to arrange guided tours and recommend local eateries. Additional details and bookings can be made through their official website: (https://www.bbcentrodigenova.it).

Palazzo Penco

Housed in a meticulously restored 17th-century building, Palazzo Penco offers a luxurious stay in the heart of Genoa's historical center. Located near the famous Aquarium of Genoa, this boutique accommodation provides an authentic experience of the city's noble past. Rooms at Palazzo Penco start at €150 per night, reflecting its upscale offerings. The palazzo boasts a range of amenities, including complimentary Wi-Fi, a sumptuous breakfast buffet, and elegantly appointed rooms with period furnishings and modern comforts. A unique feature of Palazzo Penco is its grand ballroom, often used for special events and available for guest use, adding a touch of opulence to any stay. The property also offers curated experiences such as private city tours and wine tastings, enhancing the guest experience. For more information and reservations, visit the official website: (https://www.palazzopenco.it).

La Superba Rooms & Breakfast

Situated in the vibrant district of Castelletto, La Superba Rooms & Breakfast provides a contemporary yet historic lodging experience. This boutique B&B, housed in a 19th-century building, offers rooms starting at €90 per night, combining affordability with stylish comfort. La Superba features amenities such as free Wi-Fi, air-conditioned rooms, and a delectable breakfast featuring local and organic products. The B&B's unique charm lies in its thematic rooms, each inspired by different aspects of Genoa's culture and history, creating a personalized and immersive stay for guests. Special services include personalized check-ins, tailored local guides, and the option to book private dinners featuring traditional Ligurian cuisine.Further information and bookings can be found at their official website: (https://www.lasuperbagenova.com).

CHAPTER 3
TRANSPORTATION IN GENOA

3.1 Getting to Genoa

Genoa, the capital of Liguria in Italy, is a vibrant port city known for its rich maritime history, stunning architecture, and delicious cuisine. Nestled along the Italian Riviera, it serves as a gateway to the Mediterranean and offers a charming blend of old-world charm and modern vibrancy. For travelers planning a visit, there are several convenient ways to reach Genoa, whether by air, train, or road.

Air Travel to Genoa

Flying into Genoa is a popular and efficient option for international and domestic travelers. The main airport serving the city is Genoa Cristoforo Colombo Airport (GOA), located just a few kilometers west of the city center. This well-connected airport receives flights from numerous European destinations and some intercontinental routes. Major airlines operating flights to Genoa include Alitalia, Ryanair, Lufthansa, and British Airways. Prices for tickets can vary depending on the season, with higher prices during peak tourist months in summer and lower fares during off-peak times. On average, a round-trip ticket from major European cities like London, Paris, or Berlin can range from €100 to €300. For travelers coming from North America or Asia, prices typically range from €500 to €900 for a round-trip.

Booking flights can be conveniently done through the airlines' official websites or through travel aggregators such as Skyscanner, Expedia, or Kayak. Websites like www.alitalia.com, www.ryanair.com, and www.lufthansa.com offer user-friendly interfaces for checking flight schedules, comparing prices, and making reservations. It's advisable to book tickets well in advance to secure the best rates and preferred travel dates.

Traveling to Genoa by Train

For those who prefer a scenic and relaxing journey, traveling to Genoa by train is an excellent choice. Italy's extensive railway network connects Genoa to major cities both within the country and across Europe. Trenitalia, the primary train operator in Italy, offers frequent services to and from Genoa, including high-speed trains that significantly reduce travel time. From Milan, one of the closest major cities, the train journey to Genoa takes approximately 1.5 to 2 hours, with ticket prices ranging from €20 to €50 depending on the class and type of train. From Rome, it takes around 4 to 5 hours, with prices typically between €40 and €90. International connections are also available, such as from Nice, France, which takes about 3 hours with ticket prices ranging from €30 to €70.

Tickets can be purchased online through the Trenitalia website (www.trenitalia.com) or at train stations. The website allows travelers to choose between different classes, check schedules, and even select preferred seats. It's also worth exploring options on websites like www.thetrainline.com, which aggregates train schedules and prices from various European rail operators.

Reaching Genoa by Road

Traveling to Genoa by road offers flexibility and the opportunity to enjoy the picturesque landscapes of the Italian Riviera. The city is well-connected by a network of highways and roads, making it accessible from various parts of Italy and neighboring countries. From Milan, the drive to Genoa via the A7 highway takes around 1.5 to 2 hours. If coming from Florence, the journey via the A12 highway takes approximately 3 to 3.5 hours. For travelers driving from the south, such as from Rome, the trip along the A1 and A12 highways takes around 5 to 6 hours. For those coming from France, the A10 highway provides a scenic route along the coast, with Nice being just a 2.5 to 3-hour drive away.

Additional Travel Tips

Regardless of the mode of transportation chosen, it's beneficial to familiarize yourself with a few travel tips. Ensure your travel documents are up to date, including passports and visas if required. It's also wise to check for any travel advisories or entry requirements specific to Italy, especially in light of changing health and safety protocols. For those flying into Genoa, consider arranging airport transfers in advance. Taxis, ride-sharing services, and airport shuttles are available, providing convenient options to reach your accommodation. If traveling by train, note that Genoa has two main train stations: Genova Piazza Principe and Genova Brignole. Both stations are centrally located and well-connected to public transportation networks. Driving offers the chance to explore the region at your own pace, but be prepared for narrow and winding roads, especially along the coastal areas. Parking in the city center can be challenging, so researching parking options or opting for accommodations with parking facilities can save time and stress.

3.2 Public Transportation: Buses and Metro

Genoa offers a comprehensive public transportation network that efficiently connects the city and its outskirts. Visitors to Genoa will find several modes of public transport available, including buses, a metro system, and funiculars, all designed to cater to the diverse needs of residents and tourists alike.

Buses in Genoa

The backbone of Genoa's public transport system is its extensive bus network operated by AMT Genoa (Azienda Mobilità e Trasporti). Buses in Genoa cover virtually every corner of the city, making them a convenient option for navigating both the historic city center and its suburban areas. The bus routes are well-marked with detailed maps and timetables available at most stops and online. Visitors can purchase tickets directly from authorized outlets, newsstands, and vending machines located at major bus stops. It's advisable to buy tickets before boarding as they are not typically sold on buses. Single-ride tickets are valid for a certain duration and can be used interchangeably between buses and the metro. Alternatively, daily and weekly passes provide unlimited travel within designated zones, offering flexibility and cost-effectiveness for those planning extended stays or frequent trips across the city.

Metro System in Genoa

Genoa boasts a compact metro system known as the Metropolitana di Genova, which supplements the bus network by providing rapid transit primarily along the city's east-west axis. Currently, the metro line connects Brin to Rivarolo Ligure, with plans for further expansions to enhance connectivity in the future. The metro stations are equipped with modern facilities, including ticket machines and clear signage in Italian and English, ensuring ease of use for international visitors. Tickets for the metro can be purchased at metro stations or from authorized vendors, with options ranging from single-trip tickets to multi-day passes depending on the traveler's needs. The metro is particularly convenient for commuting between major landmarks such as the Brignole Railway Station, Via XX Settembre shopping district, and the Porto Antico (Old Port), where many of Genoa's iconic attractions are located.

Funiculars

In addition to buses and the metro, Genoa features a network of funicular railways that provide scenic routes up the city's steep hillsides. The Zecca-Righi funicular, for instance, offers breathtaking views of the cityscape as it ascends to the Righi district, known for its panoramic vistas and historical charm. These funiculars not only serve as practical transport options but also serve as tourist attractions in their own right. For those looking to explore beyond the city limits, regional trains operated by Trenitalia offer connections to nearby towns and attractions such as the picturesque Cinque Terre region, renowned for its rugged coastline and colorful villages.

Navigating Genoa's Public Transport Effectively

To navigate Genoa's public transport system effectively, visitors should familiarize themselves with the city's transport maps and schedules available online or at tourist information centers. Planning routes in advance using smartphone apps like Moovit or Google Maps can also simplify travel arrangements, providing real-time updates on bus and metro timetables, delays, and alternative routes. When using buses, it's essential to signal the driver when intending to board and to exit through the front door after paying the fare or validating the ticket. For the metro, passengers should keep their tickets handy for inspection and adhere to platform safety guidelines.

3.3 Taxis and Ride-Sharing Services

When exploring Genoa, visitors have access to a variety of transportation options beyond public transit, including taxis and ride-sharing services. These services provide flexibility and convenience, particularly for travelers navigating outside regular transport hours or seeking direct routes to specific destinations.

Taxis in Genoa

Taxis in Genoa are readily available throughout the city, offering a reliable means of transportation with meters that adhere to regulated fares. Visitors can easily spot taxis at designated ranks near major transportation hubs such as airports, train stations, and popular tourist areas like Piazza De Ferrari and Porto Antico. Taxis can also be hailed on the street, although it's common practice to use designated taxi stands for convenience and safety. Several reputable taxi companies operate in Genoa, each providing a fleet of well-maintained vehicles and professional drivers. Among them are:

-Radio Taxi Genova: One of the largest taxi cooperatives in Genoa, known for its extensive coverage and efficient service. They can be contacted via their website (https://www.radiotaxigenova.com).

-Cooperativa Radio Taxi 010: Another prominent taxi service in Genoa, offering competitive rates and 24/7 availability. They are located at Piazza della Nunziata 7R, 16124 Genova GE, Italy.

-Autoradiotaxi 1965: Established in 1965, this taxi company prides itself on reliability and customer satisfaction. They can be reached online through (http://www.autoradiotaxi1965.it).

Ride-Sharing Services in Genoa

In recent years, ride-sharing services have gained popularity in Genoa, offering an alternative to traditional taxis with the convenience of booking via smartphone apps. These services are particularly favored by tech-savvy travelers for their transparent pricing and ease of use. Popular ride-sharing companies operating in Genoa include:

-Uber: Operating globally, Uber provides rides in Genoa with upfront pricing and the ability to track your ride via the app. Their website is (https://www.uber.com/cities/genoa/), where users can also download their app.

-Bolt: Formerly known as Taxify, Bolt offers competitive rates and a user-friendly app for booking rides in Genoa. Their services can be accessed via (https://bolt.eu/en/cities/genova/), website or app.

-Free Now: Formerly MyTaxi, Free Now connects users to licensed taxi drivers in Genoa, offering both traditional taxi services and ride-hailing options through their app. More information can be found at (https://free-now.com/it/).

Pricing and Additional Information

Both taxis and ride-sharing services in Genoa operate on metered fares for traditional taxis, while ride-sharing companies typically display upfront pricing based on distance and time. Visitors should note that additional charges may apply for luggage, late-night rides, and specific services like airport transfers. For those preferring cashless transactions, ride-sharing apps allow users to link credit cards or digital wallets for seamless payments. It's advisable to check the app for any current promotions or discounts, especially for first-time users or during peak travel seasons.

3.4 Car Rentals and Driving Tips

Exploring Genoa by car offers a unique opportunity to experience the city's vibrant culture and its beautiful surroundings at your own pace. Whether you are arriving for a short visit or planning a longer stay, renting a car can enhance your journey, providing the flexibility to navigate the region's stunning coastal landscapes and historic towns.

Renting a Car in Genoa

Genoa, being a central hub in the Liguria region, offers a variety of car rental options that cater to different preferences and budgets. Many international and local car rental companies have a presence in the city, making it convenient for travelers to pick up a vehicle upon arrival. Renting a car is particularly advantageous for those who wish to explore the Italian Riviera, venture into the nearby hills, or visit lesser-known attractions off the beaten path.

Major Car Rental Companies in Genoa

Here are notable car rental companies available in Genoa, each offering a range of vehicles to suit different travel needs:

Hertz: Hertz has multiple rental locations throughout Genoa, including at the Cristoforo Colombo Airport and in the city center. You can visit their website at www.hertz.com or contact them directly through their customer service. Rental prices typically start from around €30 per day, depending on the type of vehicle and duration of the rental.

Avis: Avis is situated conveniently at the Genoa Cristoforo Colombo Airport and also in various parts of the city. More information can be found on their website www.avis.com, Expect rental rates starting from approximately €25 per day, which can vary based on vehicle type and rental length.

Europcar: Europcar offers services at the Genoa Cristoforo Colombo Airport and in several locations around the city. Visit their website at www.europcar.com for more details or contact their customer service for booking inquiries. Prices generally start from about €28 per day, with adjustments based on vehicle class and rental duration.

Sixt: Sixt is accessible at the Genoa Airport and throughout the city, providing a wide range of vehicles. For further details, visit www.sixt.com. Rental prices usually begin at around €35 per day, which may vary depending on vehicle type and rental terms.

Budget: Budget has multiple rental points in Genoa, including at the airport and in city locations. More information can be accessed on their website www.budget.com. Expect rental rates to start from about €22 per day, with variations depending on vehicle and rental period.

Booking a Rental Car

Booking a rental car in Genoa is a straightforward process, whether you choose to do so online or in person. The websites of these companies provide a user-friendly platform for booking a vehicle, where you can choose the type of car, rental duration, and add-ons such as GPS navigation or additional insurance coverage. It's advisable to book in advance, especially during peak travel seasons, to ensure availability and the best rates.

Practical Tips for Driving in Genoa

Driving in Genoa offers a unique and enriching experience, although it requires careful planning due to the city's sometimes narrow and winding streets. Here are a few practical tips for navigating the city and surrounding areas:

Local Driving Rules: Familiarize yourself with Italian driving rules, including the use of seat belts, the requirement for child car seats, and the enforcement of speed limits and other road signs.

ZTL Zones: Be aware of Zona a Traffico Limitato (ZTL) zones in the city center where only authorized vehicles are allowed. Violating these zones can result in fines, so pay attention to signs and restrictions.

Parking: Parking in Genoa can be a challenge, especially in the city center. Many areas have restricted zones, and parking fees apply. Look for public parking lots or use a GPS system to locate available spaces. Some hotels offer parking facilities for their guests.

Road Conditions: The roads in and around Genoa vary, from the well-maintained highways to narrower, winding roads in the hills and coastal areas. Always check the weather conditions and road conditions before setting out.

Fuel Stations: While fuel stations are generally available, it's wise to refuel when near a station, especially if traveling in less populated areas.

3.5 Cycling and Bike Rentals

Genoa offers visitors a unique blend of history, culture, and scenic beauty. One of the best ways to explore its winding streets, historic landmarks, and stunning coastal views is by cycling. Whether you're a casual rider or a seasoned cyclist, Genoa provides numerous options for bike rentals and cycling tours to suit every preference and budget.

Bike Rental Companies in Genoa

Bike Garden Genova: Located conveniently in the heart of Genoa, Bike Garden Genova offers a wide range of bicycles for rent. From mountain bikes to electric bikes, they cater to various needs and preferences. Their rental prices start at €15 per day for standard bikes and go up depending on the type and duration of rental. For those looking to explore beyond the city, they also provide guided tours along the Ligurian coast. Website: (https://www.bikegardengenova.it).

Genoa Bike Rental: Situated near the Old Port of Genoa, Genoa Bike Rental offers both traditional bikes and electric bikes for rent. Their rental rates begin at €12 per day for standard bikes and €25 for electric bikes. They also provide helmets, locks, and maps to ensure a safe and enjoyable cycling experience through the city's historic center or along the seaside promenade. Website: (https://www.genovabikerental.it).

Bike Square: For those interested in exploring Genoa's hills and outskirts, Bike Square provides specialized mountain bikes and touring bikes. Located close to Piazza delle Erbe, they offer rentals starting at €20 per day for mountain bikes and €30 for touring bikes. They also offer repair services and cycling accessories for purchase. Website: (https://www.bikesquare.it).

Frentani Bikes: Frentani Bikes is known for its friendly service and diverse bike options. Located in the Nervi district, they offer city bikes, tandem bikes, and children's bikes at competitive rates. Rentals start at €10 per day for city bikes, making it a budget-friendly option for families and solo travelers alike. Website: (https://www.frentanibikes.it).

Bikester: Situated in the vibrant district of Albaro, Bikester caters primarily to cycling enthusiasts seeking high-performance bikes and professional gear. They offer road bikes, carbon bikes, and accessories suitable for competitive riding or long-distance tours. Prices vary based on the model and rental duration, starting from €30 per day for road bikes. Website: (https://www.bikester.it).

Exploring Genoa by Bike

Cycling in Genoa presents an excellent opportunity to discover its rich cultural heritage and natural beauty at your own pace. The city boasts a network of bike-friendly paths along the coast and through its historic neighborhoods, such as the picturesque Boccadasse and the bustling Via Garibaldi. Most bike rental companies provide maps and suggested routes, ensuring you can navigate effortlessly through the city's labyrinthine streets and scenic routes.

Tips for Cycling in Genoa

Before embarking on your cycling adventure, it's advisable to familiarize yourself with Genoa's traffic rules and cycling regulations. Helmets are not mandatory for adults but strongly recommended, especially when cycling along busy streets. Always lock your bike securely when not in use, and consider exploring the city during early mornings or late afternoons to avoid peak traffic times.

3.6 Ferries and Boat Services

Genoa, with its historic port and strategic location on the Ligurian coast, offers a vibrant array of ferry and boat services that connect the city to nearby islands, coastal towns, and other Mediterranean destinations. Whether for sightseeing, day trips, or longer journeys, these services provide visitors with unique perspectives of the region's scenic coastline and cultural heritage.

Ferry and Boat Companies in Genoa

Several reputable ferry and boat companies operate out of Genoa, each offering distinct routes, services, and amenities tailored to different traveler preferences:

-GNV (Grandi Navi Veloci): Known for its fleet of modern ferries, GNV operates routes connecting Genoa to destinations such as Sardinia, Sicily, Spain, and Tunisia. Their services cater to both passengers and vehicles, with onboard facilities including restaurants, cabins, and entertainment options. More information can be found on their website (https://www.gnv.it/en).

-Corsica Ferries: This company provides ferry services between Genoa and Corsica, offering multiple crossings per week during the peak season. Corsica Ferries emphasizes comfort and convenience with spacious seating areas, restaurants, and pet-friendly accommodations. Visit their website (https://www.corsicaferries.com), for schedules and booking details.

-Tirrenia: Operating under the Moby Group, Tirrenia connects Genoa to various destinations in Sardinia and Sicily. They offer both daytime and overnight crossings with amenities such as restaurants, bars, and comfortable cabins. For more information, visit (https://www.tirrenia.it).

-Blu Navy: Specializing in routes between Genoa and the island of Sardinia, Blu Navy provides reliable ferry services with a focus on efficiency and

affordability. Their website (https://www.blunavytraghetti.com), offers online booking options and detailed route information.

-NGI (Navigazione Generale Italiana): NGI operates ferry services from Genoa to the nearby island of Capraia, known for its natural beauty and pristine beaches. Their services cater to both tourists and locals seeking a tranquil escape from the mainland. Visit (https://www.ngi-spa.it), for schedules and ticket reservations.

Booking and Pricing

Booking ferry and boat services in Genoa can typically be done online via the respective company websites or through authorized travel agents. Prices vary depending on the route, time of year, and type of accommodation chosen (e.g., standard seating, cabins). It's advisable to book in advance, especially during peak tourist seasons, to secure preferred travel dates and amenities. Ferry ticket prices generally include the cost of transportation, but additional fees may apply for bringing vehicles onboard or opting for upgraded seating arrangements. Travelers should check the specific terms and conditions of each ferry company regarding baggage allowances, boarding procedures, and cancellation policies to ensure a smooth journey.

CHAPTER 4
TOP 10 HIDDEN GEM ATTRACTIONS

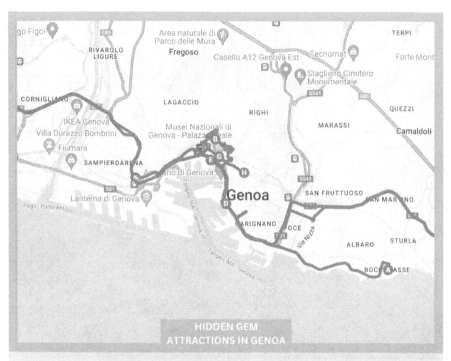

HIDDEN GEM
ATTRACTIONS IN GENOA

Directions from Boccadasse, Genoa, Metropolitan City of Genoa, Italy to Via Garibaldi, Genoa, Metropolitan City of Genoa, Italy

A
Boccadasse, Genoa, Metropolitan City of Genoa, Italy

B
Castello D'Albertis, Corso Sogali, Genoa, Metropolitan City of Genoa, Italy

C
Villa Durazzo-Pallavicini, Via Ignazio Pallavicini, Genoa, Metropolitan City of Genoa, Italy

D
Santa Maria di Castello, Salita di Santa Maria di Castello, Genoa, Metropolitan City of Genoa, Italy

E
Galata Museo del Mare, Calata Ansaldo De Mari, Genoa, Metropolitan City of Genoa

F
Passeggiata Anita Garibaldi, Genoa, Metropolitan City of Genoa, Italy

G
Musei Nazionali di Genova - Palazzo Reale, Via Balbi, Genoa, Metropolitan City of Genoa, Italy

H
Via Garibaldi, Genoa, Metropolitan City of Genoa, Italy

4.1 Boccadasse: The Seaside Village

Boccadasse, a gem along the Ligurian coast that captivates visitors with its serene beauty and rich cultural heritage. While the seaside village itself is the crown jewel, there are several other captivating places worth exploring within and around Boccadasse.

Boccadasse Beach and Promenade

The heart of Boccadasse's allure lies in its picturesque beach and charming promenade. This small pebbled beach, embraced by colorful houses and overlooked by a quaint church, offers a tranquil escape from the bustling city. Visitors can unwind on the shore, bask in the Mediterranean sun, or take leisurely strolls along the promenade lined with gelaterias and cafes offering delectable local treats.

Sant'Antonio di Boccadasse Church

Overlooking the bay of Boccadasse stands the Sant'Antonio di Boccadasse Church, a historic landmark dating back to the 12th century. This Romanesque-style church, with its distinctive bell tower and simple yet elegant façade, provides a glimpse into the village's religious heritage. Inside, visitors can admire frescoes and religious artifacts that reflect the area's cultural significance and historical evolution.

Capo Santa Chiara and Nervi Coastal Walk

For those seeking a scenic adventure, the Capo Santa Chiara and Nervi Coastal Walk offers breathtaking views of the Ligurian Sea and rugged coastline. Beginning from Boccadasse, this picturesque trail winds along cliffs adorned with Mediterranean flora, providing ample opportunities for photography and moments of serenity amidst nature's splendor. The walk leads to the neighboring district of Nervi, known for its parks, gardens, and historical villas.

Museo di Nervi - Wolfsoniana

A short distance from Boccadasse, the Museo di Nervi - Wolfsoniana beckons art enthusiasts and history buffs alike. Housed within the grand Villa Saluzzo Serra, this museum showcases a diverse collection of decorative arts, furniture, and design objects from the 19th and 20th centuries. Its meticulously curated exhibits offer insights into European artistic trends and cultural influences, making it a captivating cultural excursion from Boccadasse.

Castello d'Albertis

Perched atop a hill overlooking Genoa and its coastline, Castello d'Albertis stands as a testament to the city's maritime heritage and global connections. Built in the late 19th century by Captain Enrico Alberto d'Albertis, this castle-like structure houses the Museo delle Culture del Mondo (Museum of World Cultures), featuring artifacts and ethnographic collections from diverse civilizations across continents. The castle's panoramic views and eclectic collections make it a must-visit for history enthusiasts and panoramic views enthusiasts.

4.2 Castello d'Albertis

Perched majestically on a hill overlooking the city of Genoa and its bustling port, Castello d'Albertis stands as a testament to both architectural grandeur and the adventurous spirit of its creator, Captain Enrico Alberto d'Albertis. This unique castle-like structure, built in the late 19th century, offers visitors a captivating journey through global cultures and historical artifacts.

Museo delle Culture del Mondo (Museum of World Cultures)

The heart of Castello d'Albertis is its renowned Museum of World Cultures, a treasure trove of artifacts collected by Captain d'Albertis during his maritime expeditions. The museum's diverse exhibits span continents and centuries, showcasing ethnographic collections from Africa, Asia, Oceania, and the Americas. Visitors can explore intricately carved masks, ceremonial objects, textiles, and archaeological finds, each offering insights into the lifestyles, beliefs, and artistic traditions of cultures around the globe. The museum's thematic galleries and interactive displays provide a comprehensive understanding of human diversity and historical interconnectedness.

Tower of Castello d'Albertis

Rising above the museum is the iconic Tower of Castello d'Albertis, offering panoramic views of Genoa's cityscape, harbor, and the Ligurian Sea. Climbing to the top of the tower rewards visitors with breathtaking vistas, making it a favorite spot for photographers and history enthusiasts alike. The tower's architectural details, including battlements and medieval-inspired design elements, evoke a sense of medieval splendor against the modern backdrop of Genoa.

Historical Interiors and Decor

Within Castello d'Albertis, the interiors reflect the eclectic tastes and adventurous spirit of its original owner. Lavishly decorated rooms feature ornate ceilings, intricate woodwork, and period furnishings that transport visitors back to the late 19th century. Each room tells a story of Captain d'Albertis' voyages, with artifacts and mementos displayed alongside historical photographs and navigational instruments. The castle's interior design merges elements of Gothic, Renaissance, and Moorish styles, creating a captivating ambiance that complements its diverse collections.

Gardens of Castello d'Albertis

Surrounding Castello d'Albertis are meticulously landscaped gardens, offering tranquil spaces to relax and contemplate amidst lush greenery and panoramic views. The gardens feature Mediterranean flora, stone pathways, and shaded alcoves, inviting visitors to unwind and appreciate the castle's hilltop setting. The serene ambiance and botanical diversity make the gardens an ideal spot for leisurely strolls or quiet moments of reflection.

Educational Programs and Events

Castello d'Albertis hosts a variety of educational programs, workshops, and cultural events throughout the year, catering to visitors of all ages and interests. From guided tours exploring the museum's collections to thematic exhibitions and lectures by experts in anthropology and maritime history, the castle provides opportunities for deeper engagement with its cultural heritage. Special events such as traditional music performances, art installations, and seasonal festivals further enrich the visitor experience, fostering a dynamic dialogue between past and present.

4.3 Parco di Villa Durazzo Pallavicini

Located in Pegli, a charming district of Genoa, Parco di Villa Durazzo Pallavicini offers a captivating blend of natural beauty, historical significance, and architectural splendor. This 19th-century park, renowned for its romantic gardens and intricate landscaping, invites visitors to wander through a landscape where art, nature, and history converge harmoniously.

Villa Durazzo Pallavicini

At the heart of the park stands Villa Durazzo Pallavicini, a magnificent neoclassical villa built in the early 19th century. Designed by architect Michele Canzio, the villa's façade is adorned with Ionic columns and elaborate stucco work, embodying the grandeur of Genoese aristocratic residences of the era. Visitors can explore the villa's elegant interiors, including opulent reception rooms and historic galleries adorned with period furnishings and artworks. The villa offers a glimpse into the lifestyle of the Pallavicini family and their patronage of the arts during the Romantic period.

Romantic Gardens

The park is renowned for its meticulously landscaped Romantic gardens, which encompass a variety of themed areas inspired by different cultures and historical periods. Visitors can stroll along winding pathways bordered by ancient trees, tranquil ponds, and vibrant flower beds. Highlights include the Oriental garden with exotic plants, the English garden with its naturalistic layout, and the Italian garden featuring formal terraces and statuesque fountains. Each garden area offers a unique ambiance and opportunities for relaxation amidst lush greenery and picturesque vistas.

Labyrinth

A central feature of Parco di Villa Durazzo Pallavicini is its intricate labyrinth, designed in the early 19th century as a playful and contemplative space. The labyrinth's geometric layout of high hedges and winding paths provides an engaging challenge for visitors of all ages. Navigating through the labyrinth leads to a central pavilion, offering a moment of reflection amidst the park's enchanting surroundings. The labyrinth symbolizes the park's dedication to both aesthetic beauty and intellectual curiosity, making it a must-see attraction within Villa Durazzo Pallavicini.

Temple of Diana

Overlooking the park's expansive lawns and gardens stands the Temple of Diana, a neoclassical pavilion inspired by ancient Roman architecture. Built as a place of contemplation and admiration for nature, the temple features Doric columns, a pediment adorned with sculptures, and panoramic views of the surrounding landscape. The Temple of Diana serves as a focal point for visitors seeking tranquility and panoramic views of the park, providing a serene retreat amidst its verdant surroundings.

Historical Arboretum

Parco di Villa Durazzo Pallavicini is home to an extensive arboretum showcasing a diverse collection of rare and exotic trees from around the world. The arboretum's botanical diversity includes species such as sequoias, magnolias, and palms, each carefully cultivated to thrive in Genoa's Mediterranean climate. Visitors can embark on botanical tours to learn about the park's conservation efforts and the ecological significance of its plant species. The arboretum offers a serene setting for nature enthusiasts and provides educational opportunities for understanding the importance of biodiversity and environmental stewardship.

4.4 Santa Maria di Castello

Santa Maria di Castello stands as a testament to the city's rich religious heritage and architectural splendor. This complex, comprising a church, cloisters, and museum, offers visitors a glimpse into centuries of Genoese history, art, and culture.

Santa Maria di Castello Church

The centerpiece of the complex is the Santa Maria di Castello Church, originally built in the 12th century and subsequently renovated and expanded over the centuries. The church showcases a harmonious blend of Romanesque and Gothic architectural styles, characterized by its robust columns, elegant arches, and intricately carved details. Inside, visitors can admire impressive frescoes, ornate altars, and sculptures depicting religious scenes, reflecting the artistic achievements and spiritual devotion of Genoese craftsmen throughout the ages.

Cloisters of Santa Maria di Castello

Adjacent to the church are the tranquil Cloisters of Santa Maria di Castello, a serene oasis adorned with colonnades, ancient columns, and a central garden. Originally serving as a place of contemplation for monks, the cloisters feature elegant Gothic arches and Renaissance elements, creating a peaceful atmosphere ideal for reflection and photography. Visitors can wander through the cloisters, enjoying the interplay of light and shadow amidst centuries-old architectural beauty.

Museo Diocesano di Genova (Diocesan Museum of Genoa)

Located within the complex is the Museo Diocesano di Genova, housed in the former convent of Santa Maria di Castello. The museum showcases a rich collection of religious art and artifacts spanning from the medieval period to the Baroque era. Highlights include precious liturgical objects, illuminated manuscripts, paintings by renowned Genoese artists, and religious sculptures that provide insights into Genoa's cultural and spiritual heritage. The museum's exhibits offer a comprehensive overview of the evolution of religious art and the role of Christianity in shaping Genoese society.

Oratory of Santa Caterina

Within the Santa Maria di Castello complex, visitors can explore the Oratory of Santa Caterina, a hidden gem renowned for its exquisite frescoes and historical significance. The oratory, dating back to the 14th century, features stunning frescoes depicting scenes from the life of Saint Catherine of Alexandria, painted by prominent Genoese artists. The intimate setting of the oratory allows visitors to appreciate the artistry and religious devotion that characterized Genoa during the Renaissance period.

Archaeological Area and Ancient Crypt

Beneath the Santa Maria di Castello complex lies an archaeological area and ancient crypt, offering a fascinating glimpse into Genoa's early history. The archaeological excavations have revealed remnants of Roman structures and medieval foundations, shedding light on the city's evolution from ancient times to the Middle Ages. Visitors can explore these underground chambers and learn about the archaeological discoveries that have uncovered layers of Genoa's past, adding depth to their understanding of the city's cultural heritage.

4.5 Galata Museo del Mare

Galata Museo del Mare (Galata Museum of the Sea) is a captivating tribute to the city's rich maritime history and global seafaring legacy. This dynamic museum complex offers an immersive journey through centuries of naval exploration, trade, and cultural exchange.

Exhibition Halls

Galata Museo del Mare boasts extensive exhibition halls showcasing a diverse array of maritime artifacts, models of historic ships, navigational instruments, and interactive displays. Visitors can delve into the maritime traditions of Genoa, from its origins as a powerful maritime republic to its role in the Age of Exploration and beyond. The exhibitions highlight the city's maritime prowess, trade routes, naval battles, and technological advancements that shaped global maritime history. Interactive exhibits engage visitors of all ages, offering hands-on experiences and multimedia presentations that bring the maritime world to life.

The Real Galata

One of the museum's standout attractions is the full-scale replica of the Galata, a 17th-century galleon that offers visitors a glimpse into the life aboard a historic ship. This meticulously reconstructed vessel allows visitors to explore the decks, cabins, and crew quarters, experiencing firsthand the challenges and adventures faced by sailors during the Age of Sail. Guided tours provide insights into maritime navigation, daily routines onboard, and the historical significance of ships like the Galata in global trade and exploration.

Submarine Nazario Sauro

An intriguing feature of Galata Museo del Mare is the Submarine Nazario Sauro, a decommissioned Italian Navy submarine permanently docked adjacent to the museum. Visitors can embark on guided tours inside the submarine, discovering its cramped quarters, control room, and operational equipment. The submarine tour offers a unique perspective on underwater warfare technology and the daily life of submariners, highlighting Italy's naval defense history and technological innovations in maritime warfare.

Virtual Reality Experiences

Galata Museo del Mare offers innovative virtual reality experiences that transport visitors to pivotal moments in maritime history. Through immersive VR simulations, visitors can navigate historic ships, explore distant ports of call, and witness significant maritime events firsthand. These virtual journeys provide a dynamic and educational perspective on the realities of seafaring life and the global impact of maritime exploration and trade routes.

Educational Programs and Workshops

The museum hosts a variety of educational programs, workshops, and activities designed to engage visitors of all ages. From maritime-themed workshops for children to lectures by historians and maritime experts, Galata Museo del Mare offers opportunities for learning and discovery. Special events, including maritime festivals, historical reenactments, and temporary exhibitions, enrich the visitor experience by celebrating Genoa's maritime heritage and cultural diversity.

4.6 Passeggiata Anita Garibaldi a Nervi

Stretching along the rugged coastline of Nervi, a charming district of Genoa, Passeggiata Anita Garibaldi offers visitors a picturesque blend of natural beauty, historical landmarks, and panoramic views of the Ligurian Sea. Named after Anita Garibaldi, the wife and comrade-in-arms of Italian revolutionary Giuseppe Garibaldi, this scenic promenade invites visitors to explore its captivating attractions and enjoy moments of tranquility by the sea.

Villa Grimaldi Fassio

The promenade begins at Villa Grimaldi Fassio, a historic villa dating back to the 17th century. Surrounded by lush gardens overlooking the sea, this elegant villa showcases Genoese architecture and serves as the gateway to Passeggiata Anita Garibaldi. Visitors can admire the villa's facade, stroll through its gardens, and enjoy panoramic views of the coastline, making it an ideal starting point for a leisurely walk along the promenade.

Park of Nervi

Adjacent to Passeggiata Anita Garibaldi lies the expansive Park of Nervi, a verdant oasis boasting botanical gardens, Mediterranean flora, and scenic pathways. The park offers a serene escape from the city's hustle and bustle, inviting visitors to explore its shaded trails, blooming flower beds, and charming ponds. Highlights include the Rose Garden with its vibrant blooms, the Olive Grove offering panoramic vistas, and the Archaeological Museum of Nervi, showcasing Roman artifacts amidst tranquil surroundings.

Anita Garibaldi Promenade

Named in honor of Anita Garibaldi, the Anita Garibaldi Promenade winds along the rugged coastline of Nervi, offering stunning views of the Ligurian Sea and rocky cliffs. The promenade's well-maintained pathways are perfect for leisurely walks or bicycle rides, providing ample opportunities for photography and relaxation amidst nature's splendor. Visitors can pause at scenic overlooks, enjoy sea breezes, and soak in the timeless beauty of the Mediterranean coastline.

Nervi Marinas and Seafront

As visitors continue along Passeggiata Anita Garibaldi, they encounter charming marinas and quaint seafront cafes dotted along the coastline. The marinas host colorful fishing boats and yachts, adding a maritime charm to the promenade's ambiance. Visitors can savor fresh seafood at waterfront restaurants, explore local artisan shops, or simply admire the maritime activity unfolding along the shoreline. The seafront offers a vibrant glimpse into Nervi's coastal lifestyle and provides opportunities to experience Genoa's maritime traditions firsthand.

Porticciolo Capolungo

At the conclusion of Passeggiata Anita Garibaldi stands Porticciolo Capolungo, a historic harbor dating back to the 18th century. This picturesque port features traditional Ligurian architecture, including colorful fishermen's houses and a quaint chapel overlooking the sea. Visitors can wander through the harbor, watch fishermen at work, or enjoy a peaceful moment by the water's edge. Porticciolo Capolungo encapsulates the maritime heritage of Nervi and serves as a charming conclusion to the scenic journey along Passeggiata Anita Garibaldi.

4.7 Museo di Palazzo Reale

Situated in the heart of Genoa's historic center, Museo di Palazzo Reale (Royal Palace Museum) offers visitors a compelling glimpse into the city's rich cultural heritage, aristocratic legacy, and artistic treasures. Housed within the opulent Palazzo Reale, this museum complex showcases centuries of Genoese history through its magnificent architecture, royal apartments, and extensive collections of art and artifacts.

Palazzo Reale

The centerpiece of the museum is Palazzo Reale itself, a magnificent palace dating back to the 17th century and once the residence of the Doges of Genoa. Designed by architect Bartolomeo Bianco, the palace features grand halls, ornate staircases, and opulent salons adorned with frescoes, stuccoes, and period furnishings. Visitors can explore the palace's lavish interiors, including the Throne Room, Ballroom, and Royal Chapel, which exemplify Genoa's aristocratic splendor and cultural refinement during the Baroque era.

National Gallery

The National Gallery within Museo di Palazzo Reale houses an impressive collection of paintings, sculptures, and decorative arts spanning from the medieval period to the 19th century. Highlights include works by renowned Genoese artists such as Bernardo Strozzi, Luca Cambiaso, and Giovanni Benedetto Castiglione, showcasing the city's artistic achievements and regional influences. The gallery's diverse exhibits provide insights into Genoa's role as a center of artistic innovation and cultural exchange throughout history.

Royal Apartments

Visitors can explore the sumptuous Royal Apartments of Palazzo Reale, where the Doges and their families once resided in regal splendor. The apartments feature intricately decorated rooms furnished with period furnishings, tapestries, and priceless artworks. Each room offers a glimpse into courtly life and ceremonial rituals of Genoa's noble elite, illustrating the palace's significance as a political and cultural center during the Renaissance and Baroque periods.

Gardens of Palazzo Reale

Adjacent to Palazzo Reale are the tranquil Gardens of Palazzo Reale, a verdant oasis amidst the bustling city center. Designed in the Italian Renaissance style, the gardens feature manicured lawns, elegant fountains, and sculpted hedges, providing a serene retreat for visitors to unwind and appreciate the palace's architectural beauty. The gardens offer panoramic views of Genoa's historic skyline and serve as a peaceful respite from exploring the museum's cultural treasures.

Temporary Exhibitions and Cultural Events

Museo di Palazzo Reale hosts a vibrant program of temporary exhibitions, cultural events, and educational activities throughout the year. From themed exhibitions showcasing specific artists or historical periods to concerts, lectures, and theatrical performances, the museum offers opportunities for visitors to engage with Genoa's cultural heritage in dynamic and immersive ways. Special events celebrate the city's artistic legacy, culinary traditions, and maritime history, enriching the visitor experience and fostering a deeper appreciation for Genoa's multifaceted identity.

4.8 Via Garibaldi and the Palazzi dei Rolli

Located in the heart of Genoa's historic center, Via Garibaldi and the Palazzi dei Rolli represent a remarkable ensemble of Renaissance and Baroque architecture, showcasing the city's wealth, cultural prominence, and architectural innovation during the 16th and 17th centuries. This UNESCO World Heritage Site invites visitors to wander through a labyrinth of majestic palaces, elegant courtyards, and opulent interiors, offering a glimpse into Genoa's golden age as a powerful maritime republic.

Palazzo Rosso

One of the prominent palaces along Via Garibaldi is Palazzo Rosso, renowned for its stunning façade adorned with frescoes and architectural details. This Baroque palace houses an impressive art collection, featuring works by renowned artists such as Van Dyck, Veronese, and Guercino. Visitors can explore lavishly decorated rooms, including the noble floor with its sumptuous salons, period furnishings, and ornate ceilings. Palazzo Rosso offers a comprehensive overview of Genoa's artistic heritage and aristocratic lifestyle during the Baroque era.

Palazzo Bianco

Adjacent to Palazzo Rosso is Palazzo Bianco, another jewel of Genoa's architectural and artistic heritage. This palace showcases an extensive collection of European paintings from the 15th to the 18th centuries, including masterpieces by Caravaggio, Rubens, and Van Dyck. Palazzo Bianco's elegant interiors feature intricate stuccoes, marble floors, and period furniture, providing a rich backdrop for the museum's exceptional art collection. The palace offers a compelling narrative of Genoa's cultural patronage and artistic achievements during the Renaissance and Baroque periods.

Palazzo Doria Tursi

Further along Via Garibaldi stands Palazzo Doria Tursi, an imposing Renaissance palace that once belonged to the influential Doria family. The palace is renowned for its grand façade adorned with marble columns, sculpted reliefs, and a monumental staircase. Visitors can explore the palace's opulent rooms, which house the municipal collections of Genoa, including historical artifacts, musical instruments, and a notable violin collection. Palazzo Doria

Tursi provides insights into Genoa's civic history and cultural heritage through its impressive architecture and eclectic collections.

Courtyards and Loggias

Via Garibaldi is lined with interconnected courtyards and loggias that enhance the architectural charm of the Palazzi dei Rolli. These elegant spaces feature Renaissance arcades, sculpted columns, and intricate decorations, creating inviting settings for leisurely strolls and architectural appreciation. Visitors can admire the harmonious blend of public and private spaces, imagining the bustling social gatherings and diplomatic ceremonies that once animated these historic palaces. The courtyards and loggias exemplify Genoa's urban planning and architectural sophistication during its heyday as a leading European port city.

Museums and Cultural Events

Via Garibaldi and the Palazzi dei Rolli host a variety of cultural events, exhibitions, and guided tours throughout the year. From themed museum exhibitions exploring art and history to cultural festivals celebrating Genoa's culinary traditions and musical heritage, the area offers opportunities for visitors to engage with its vibrant cultural scene. Special events often include open-air concerts, historical reenactments, and theatrical performances that animate the palaces and courtyards, providing immersive experiences that bring Genoa's Renaissance splendor to life.

4.9 Genoa's Secret Gardens

The city's secret gardens offer tranquil escapes and verdant oases amidst the bustling urban landscape. These hidden gems, often tucked away behind ancient walls or concealed within private residences, invite visitors to discover their botanical diversity, historical significance, and serene atmospheres.

Orto Botanico

Located in the heart of Genoa's historic center, Orto Botanico is a botanical garden dating back to the 19th century. This hidden gem features a rich collection of plants, trees, and medicinal herbs, organized according to their geographic origins and botanical classifications. Visitors can explore themed sections such as the Mediterranean garden, succulent collection, and aromatic herb beds, each offering educational insights into plant diversity and conservation. Orto Botanico provides a peaceful retreat for nature enthusiasts and botany lovers alike, showcasing Genoa's commitment to preserving botanical heritage within an urban setting.

Giardino Flora Tropicale

Tucked away in a secluded corner of Genoa's hillsides, Giardino Flora Tropicale is a tropical botanical garden renowned for its exotic plants and lush greenery. This secret garden features a diverse array of tropical and subtropical species, including palms, orchids, and rare flowering trees. Visitors can wander along shaded pathways, discover hidden water features, and marvel at vibrant blooms amidst a tranquil ambiance reminiscent of faraway rainforests. Giardino Flora Tropicale offers a sensory journey into the biodiversity of tropical climates, making it a unique and memorable destination in Genoa's botanical landscape.

Villa Durazzo-Pallavicini Gardens

Although not entirely hidden, Villa Durazzo-Pallavicini Gardens in Pegli offers a captivating blend of historical architecture and landscaped gardens that feel like a secret paradise. Designed in the Romantic style during the 19th century, these gardens feature winding paths, ornamental lakes, and picturesque follies nestled amidst towering trees and colorful flower beds. Visitors can explore themed areas such as the Oriental garden, English landscape garden, and Italian terraces, each offering panoramic views of the Ligurian Sea and opportunities for contemplation and relaxation.

Giardino della Lanterna

Adjacent to the iconic Lanterna lighthouse, Giardino della Lanterna is a hidden botanical gem dedicated to showcasing native Mediterranean flora. This garden celebrates Genoa's maritime heritage and environmental stewardship, featuring drought-resistant plants, aromatic herbs, and maritime species adapted to the region's coastal climate. Visitors can enjoy panoramic views of the harbor, explore educational exhibits on maritime botany, and participate in guided tours highlighting the ecological significance of preserving coastal ecosystems. Giardino della Lanterna offers a serene retreat for nature lovers and a glimpse into Genoa's commitment to sustainability and biodiversity conservation.

Palazzo Reale Gardens

Within the grounds of Palazzo Reale, adjacent to Via Balbi, are the charming Palazzo Reale Gardens, a tranquil haven amidst the city's historic center. These gardens feature sculpted hedges, manicured lawns, and shaded pergolas adorned with climbing roses and fragrant jasmine. Visitors can unwind amidst classical statues, ornamental fountains, and centuries-old trees, soaking in the serene ambiance and enjoying views of the palace's majestic façade. Palazzo Reale Gardens offer a peaceful respite from urban bustle, inviting visitors to appreciate

Genoa's architectural and botanical heritage in a secluded and timeless setting.

4.10 The Ancient Walls and Fortresses

Genoa's ancient walls and fortresses stand as formidable monuments to the city's strategic importance and military prowess throughout its storied history. These architectural marvels, dating from medieval times to the Renaissance era, offer visitors a glimpse into Genoa's defensive strategies, urban development, and cultural heritage. From panoramic views of the cityscape to immersive historical experiences, exploring the ancient walls and fortresses of Genoa promises a journey through time and a deeper understanding of its enduring significance.

Porta Soprana and the Medieval Walls

Porta Soprana is a striking gateway that once served as the main entrance to medieval Genoa. Constructed in the 12th century, this fortified gate is flanked by two massive towers and offers a glimpse into Genoa's medieval defensive architecture. Visitors can climb to the top of the towers for panoramic views of the city and explore the adjacent sections of the medieval city walls that once encircled Genoa, marveling at their sturdy construction and historical significance in defending the city against invaders.

Castello d'Albertis

Perched atop a hill overlooking Genoa's historic port district, Castello d'Albertis is a distinctive fortress that blends medieval and Moorish architectural styles. Built in the late 19th century by Captain Enrico Alberto d'Albertis, an avid explorer and collector, the castle houses a fascinating museum showcasing artifacts and ethnographic collections from around the world. Visitors can explore the castle's towers, battlements, and panoramic terraces, enjoying sweeping views of the cityscape and the Ligurian Sea while delving into the adventurous spirit of its founder.

Forte Sperone

Forte Sperone, located on a hillside overlooking the city center, is a well-preserved fortress dating back to the 16th century. This imposing structure was part of Genoa's extensive defensive network, designed to protect the city from maritime threats and land invasions. Visitors can tour the fortress's bastions, barracks, and underground tunnels, gaining insights into military architecture and tactics during the Renaissance period. The panoramic views from Forte Sperone offer a dramatic backdrop for exploring Genoa's historical landscape and appreciating its strategic importance as a maritime republic.

Forte Diamante

Located on the eastern outskirts of Genoa, Forte Diamante is a star-shaped fortress built in the 18th century to defend the city from potential attacks from the sea. This well-preserved fortress features a series of interconnected bastions, casemates, and artillery platforms designed to withstand naval bombardments and ground assaults. Visitors can explore the fortress's interior, including its powder magazines and defensive walls, and learn about its role in Genoa's maritime defense strategies. The strategic location of Forte Diamante offers commanding views of the Ligurian coastline, providing a glimpse into Genoa's historical maritime defenses.

Forte San Giuliano

Forte San Giuliano, perched on a hill overlooking Genoa's western suburbs, is a 19th-century fortress that played a crucial role in the city's coastal defense system. Designed in response to technological advancements in artillery and warfare, the fortress features imposing ramparts, artillery batteries, and underground galleries. Visitors can explore the fortress's labyrinthine passages, artillery emplacements, and panoramic viewpoints, gaining insights into Genoa's military history and its efforts to protect its maritime interests. Forte San Giuliano offers a blend of historical exploration and scenic beauty, inviting visitors to appreciate Genoa's strategic defenses and panoramic vistas of the city and sea.

4.11 Sports, Outdoor Activities and Adventures

Genoa, the vibrant port city on the northwest coast of Italy, offers a plethora of sports, outdoor activities, and adventures amidst its rich historical backdrop and stunning natural landscapes. From sea-based escapades to mountainous hikes, Genoa caters to a diverse range of outdoor enthusiasts seeking both adrenaline-pumping experiences and serene natural beauty.

Sailing and Boating in the Ligurian Sea

One of the quintessential experiences in Genoa is sailing or boating along the Ligurian Sea, known for its crystal-clear waters and picturesque coastline. Several tour operators offer sailing excursions that depart from Genoa's historic Old Port (Porto Antico). Visitors can choose from day trips to multi-day sailing adventures, exploring charming seaside villages like Camogli and Portofino along the way. Prices for these tours vary depending on the duration and type of vessel, with options ranging from luxurious yachts to more affordable sailboats. Special services often include onboard dining featuring local cuisine and opportunities for swimming and snorkeling in secluded coves.

Hiking in the Ligurian Mountains

For those who prefer exploring on foot, the Ligurian Mountains offer an extensive network of hiking trails just a short distance from the bustling city center of Genoa. The trails wind through lush forests, past ancient villages clinging to hilltops, and offer breathtaking panoramic views of the Mediterranean coastline. Guided hiking tours are available for all skill levels, from leisurely walks suitable for families to challenging treks for experienced hikers. Tour prices generally include transportation to and from Genoa, knowledgeable guides who provide insights into the region's flora, fauna, and history, and sometimes picnic lunches featuring local delicacies.

Cycling along the Riviera dei Fiori

Cycling enthusiasts can enjoy exploring the Riviera dei Fiori (Riviera of Flowers), a scenic coastal route that stretches from Genoa to the French border. This cycling paradise offers diverse landscapes ranging from rugged cliffs to sandy beaches, with charming towns and villages dotted along the way. Bike rental shops in Genoa provide a range of bicycles suitable for various terrains, including mountain bikes for more adventurous cyclists. Guided cycling tours often include support vehicles, accommodation arrangements, and optional gourmet food and wine tastings at local vineyards.

Rock Climbing in the Apennine Mountains

For adrenaline seekers, the Apennine Mountains near Genoa offer excellent opportunities for rock climbing and mountaineering. Guided rock climbing tours cater to both beginners looking to learn basic techniques and experienced climbers seeking challenging ascents. The rugged cliffs and limestone crags of the Apennines provide a thrilling backdrop for climbers, with routes varying in difficulty to suit different skill levels.

Kayaking in the Gulf of Tigullio

Exploring the Gulf of Tigullio by kayak offers a unique perspective of Genoa's coastal beauty, combining adventure with opportunities for wildlife spotting and secluded beach exploration. Kayak rental companies provide single and tandem kayaks along with safety equipment and briefings on paddling techniques. Guided kayak tours lead paddlers through marine reserves and along rugged coastlines, with stops for snorkeling in pristine waters and picnicking on secluded beaches accessible only by sea.

4.12 Recommended Tour Operators and Guided Tours

Genoa stands as a gateway to Italy's rich maritime heritage, offering visitors a blend of historical marvels, culinary delights, and vibrant local culture. For travelers seeking to delve deeper into this captivating city, guided tours provided by seasoned operators offer an invaluable experience. These tours not only unravel the layers of Genoa's past but also provide insights into its modern charm, ensuring every visitor can savor the essence of this enchanting destination.

Walks of Italy - Genoa Tours

Located centrally, Walks of Italy offers meticulously crafted tours that unveil the essence of Genoa's history and culture. Their expert guides lead small groups through the narrow alleys of the historic center, sharing anecdotes about the city's maritime prowess and architectural heritage. Unique features include skip-the-line access to major attractions such as the Palazzi dei Rolli and the Genoa Aquarium, allowing visitors to maximize their exploration time. Prices typically range from €50 to €100 per person depending on the tour duration and inclusions. Special services like private tours and customized itineraries are available upon request. For more information, visit their official website at walksofitaly.com.

Genova More Than This

Genova More Than This stands out for its commitment to sustainable tourism and personalized experiences. Based in the heart of the old town, this operator offers thematic tours focusing on Genoa's culinary traditions, art scene, and lesser-known historical landmarks. Prices start from €40 per person for group tours, with options for private tours at higher rates. Special services include exclusive access to artisan workshops and tastings of local specialties like focaccia and pesto. Their website, genovamorethanthis.com, provides detailed itineraries and booking information tailored to diverse interests.

Discover Genoa

Catering to both first-time visitors and seasoned travelers, Discover Genoa provides a range of guided tours designed to showcase the city's hidden gems and cultural diversity. Their knowledgeable guides lead immersive walking tours through Genoa's labyrinthine streets, offering insights into its Renaissance palaces, Baroque churches, and vibrant markets. Tour prices vary from €30 to €80 per person, with family-friendly options and discounts for students. Exclusive services such as yacht tours along the coast and sunset cruises enhance the experience. Visit discovergenoa.com for tour schedules and additional details.

Genoa Free Tour

Ideal for budget-conscious travelers, Genoa Free Tour offers insightful walking tours led by local guides who are passionate about sharing their city's history. Operating on a tips-only basis, these tours provide a comprehensive overview of Genoa's landmarks including the Cathedral of San Lorenzo and the Piazza De Ferrari. While the tour itself is free, tips are appreciated and support the guides' dedication. Additional services such as private group tours and thematic itineraries can be arranged upon request. Check genoafreetour.com for tour times and meeting points.

Made in Liguria

For those seeking an off-the-beaten-path experience, Made in Liguria specializes in bespoke tours that highlight Genoa's artisanal craftsmanship and scenic surroundings. Their curated itineraries often include visits to local workshops producing traditional ceramics, textiles, and confectionery. Prices are tailored based on the specific tour requests, starting approximately from €80 per person for half-day excursions. Detailed tour descriptions and booking options can be found at madeinliguria.com.

CHAPTER 5
PRACTICAL INFORMATION AND TRAVEL RESOURCES

MAP OF GENOA

SCAN THE QR CODE WITH A DEVICE TO VIEW A COMPREHENSIVE AND LARGER MAP OF GENOA

5.1 Maps and Navigation

Navigating and exploring Genoa, a vibrant city on Italy's northwest coast, is made infinitely easier with the aid of maps and navigation tools, both traditional and digital. Whether you prefer the tangible reliability of a paper map or the convenience of a digital interface, Genoa caters to all preferences, ensuring you make the most of your visit.

Discovering Genoa through Tourist Maps

When you first arrive in Genoa, one of the most essential tools at your disposal is the tourist map. These maps are typically available at hotels, tourist information centers, and sometimes even at major attractions. They provide a comprehensive overview of the city's layout, highlighting key landmarks, neighborhoods, transportation hubs, and important points of interest such as museums, churches, and parks. A good tourist map not only helps you navigate the city efficiently but also enhances your understanding of Genoa's rich cultural and historical heritage.

Accessing Offline Maps in Genoa

For travelers who prefer the reliability of offline navigation, acquiring a physical map of Genoa is highly recommended. These maps are often detailed, foldable, and compact, making them easy to carry around. You can find them at bookstores, newsstands, and sometimes even at the airport or train stations. They are invaluable for exploring the narrow alleys of the Old Town (Centro Storico), finding hidden gems in the city's diverse neighborhoods, and understanding the public transportation routes.

Embracing Digital Navigation Tools

Genoa has become even more convenient with a plethora of digital mapping options. Most smartphones offer built-in map applications that provide real-time navigation, directions, and even public transit information. Additionally, there are several dedicated apps such as Google Maps, Apple Maps, and specialized travel apps that offer detailed maps of Genoa with features like offline mode, points of interest, and user reviews.

How to Access Genoa's Digital Maps

Accessing Genoa's digital maps is straightforward and highly accessible to anyone with a smartphone or internet-connected device. Simply download a mapping app of your choice from your device's app store. These apps typically offer both online and offline modes, allowing you to navigate even without a data connection once you've downloaded the map beforehand. This is particularly useful when exploring areas with limited internet coverage or when avoiding roaming charges.

Utilizing QR Codes for Seamless Access

To streamline the process of accessing Genoa's digital maps, many guidebooks, brochures, and tourist information centers provide QR codes or direct links. These QR codes can be scanned with your smartphone camera, instantly directing you to a comprehensive map of Genoa online. This method ensures that you always have the latest information at your fingertips, including updated points of interest, restaurant recommendations, and current events happening around the city.

Additional Tips for Visitors

When navigating Genoa, it's helpful to keep a few additional tips in mind:

-Public Transportation: Genoa has an efficient network of buses and a metro line, which are well-integrated into digital maps and provide an excellent way to explore beyond the city center.

-Walking Tours: Many attractions in Genoa are best explored on foot, and digital maps can guide you along recommended walking routes.

-Language Considerations: While digital maps are typically available in multiple languages, having a basic understanding of Italian can be advantageous when interacting with locals or navigating older parts of the city.

5.2 Seven Days Itinerary

Upon arrival in Genoa, commonly known as the gateway to the Italian Riviera, immerse yourself in its rich history and maritime heritage. Start your journey by visiting the historic center, a UNESCO World Heritage site, characterized by narrow streets (caruggi), bustling squares, and magnificent Renaissance palaces. Wander through Via Garibaldi, also known as the "Street of the Palaces," where you can admire impressive buildings such as Palazzo Rosso and Palazzo Bianco, which house renowned art collections.

Day 2: Discovering Genoa's Maritime Legacy

Dedicate your second day to exploring Genoa's maritime legacy. Begin at the Porto Antico (Old Port), revamped by renowned architect Renzo Piano. Here, visit the Aquarium of Genoa, one of Europe's largest aquariums, showcasing a diverse range of marine life. Next, explore the Galata Maritime Museum, where exhibits narrate Genoa's maritime history and its impact on global trade. Complete your day with a stroll along the waterfront, enjoying views of the harbor and the city skyline.

Day 3: Art and Culture in Genoa

Delve into Genoa's art and cultural scene on your third day. Start with a visit to the Genoa Cathedral (Cattedrale di San Lorenzo), an architectural masterpiece with a black-and-white striped facade. Inside, marvel at its frescoes and the Chapel of St. John the Baptist, home to the saint's relics. Afterwards, explore the Palazzo Ducale, once the residence of the Doges of Genoa, now a cultural center hosting art exhibitions and events. End your day with a leisurely walk in the

Piazza De Ferrari, the city's main square, surrounded by grand buildings and the iconic fountain.

Day 4: Day Trip to Cinque Terre

Take a break from the city and embark on a day trip to Cinque Terre, a UNESCO World Heritage site renowned for its picturesque coastal villages. Travel by train from Genoa to Monterosso al Mare, the largest of the five villages. Spend your day hiking along the scenic trails that connect the villages, exploring charming streets, and enjoying local cuisine such as seafood pasta and pesto, a regional specialty. Return to Genoa in the evening, reflecting on the beauty of the Ligurian coastline.

Day 5: Culinary Delights of Genoa

Indulge in Genoa's culinary delights on your fifth day. Start your gastronomic journey with a visit to Mercato Orientale, a bustling food market offering a variety of fresh produce, seafood, and local delicacies. Join a cooking class to learn how to prepare traditional Ligurian dishes such as focaccia and trofie al pesto. Alternatively, sample these delicacies at local trattorias and restaurants scattered throughout the city. In the evening, savor a gelato while strolling along the Corso Italia promenade, overlooking the sea.

Day 6: Hidden Gems and Local Experiences

Uncover Genoa's hidden gems and immerse yourself in local experiences on your sixth day. Explore the district of Boccadasse, a quaint fishing village nestled within the city, known for its colorful buildings and small beach. Visit the Museo di Sant'Agostino, a lesser-known museum showcasing archaeological finds and medieval artifacts. Alternatively, take a guided tour of the Palazzi dei Rolli, a collection of palaces that hosted important guests during the Renaissance. End your day with an aperitivo at a rooftop bar, enjoying panoramic views of the cityscape.

Day 7: Relaxation and Reflection

On your final day in Genoa, take the opportunity to relax and reflect on your experiences. Spend the morning at Villa Durazzo Pallavicini in nearby Pegli, a stunning 19th-century park featuring botanical gardens, ornate fountains, and picturesque paths. Alternatively, unwind at the Bagni Medusa or Bagni Lido, historic seaside bathing establishments where locals and visitors alike come to enjoy the sun and sea. In the afternoon, stroll through the picturesque district of Castelletto, known for its panoramic viewpoints offering sweeping vistas of Genoa and the Ligurian Sea. As evening falls, enjoy a farewell dinner at a traditional trattoria, reminiscing about your memorable week in this vibrant city.

5.3 Essential Packing List

Planning a visit to Genoa, the vibrant port city nestled along Italy's Ligurian coast, requires careful consideration of what to pack to ensure a smooth and enjoyable experience. As you prepare for your journey to this historic city steeped in maritime heritage and Renaissance charm, thoughtful packing can enhance your exploration of its winding streets, bustling markets, and architectural wonders. From climate considerations to cultural nuances, here's a guide to packing essentials that will equip you for an enriching adventure in Genoa.

Clothing Essentials

When preparing for a trip to Genoa, consider the city's Mediterranean climate. Summers are typically warm and humid, so pack lightweight and breathable clothing such as shorts, t-shirts, and dresses. Don't forget to bring comfortable walking shoes as Genoa's historic center and its charming cobblestone streets are best explored on foot. A light jacket or sweater is advisable even in summer as evenings can be cooler. If visiting during spring or autumn, pack layers to accommodate fluctuating temperatures. In winter, although mild compared to northern Europe, a heavier coat and warmer clothing are necessary.

Footwear

Comfortable walking shoes are essential for exploring Genoa's diverse neighborhoods and historical sites. Opt for sturdy yet comfortable shoes suitable for walking on uneven terrain and cobblestone streets. If planning to visit churches or museums, consider bringing a pair of comfortable dress shoes suitable for such occasions.

Travel Documents and Money

Ensure you have your passport, visa (if required), travel insurance documents, and any necessary identification readily accessible. It's prudent to carry copies of important documents stored separately from the originals. Also, remember to bring local currency (Euros) or a credit/debit card widely accepted in Italy. Inform your bank of your travel plans to avoid any issues with card usage abroad.

Electronics and Chargers

Pack your smartphone and/or camera to capture the beauty of Genoa's architecture and landscapes. Bring chargers and adapters suitable for Italian electrical outlets (Type F sockets). It's also useful to have a power bank for recharging devices on the go, especially during long days of sightseeing.

Health and Personal Care Items

Include any prescription medications you require, ensuring you have enough for the duration of your stay. Pack sunscreen and sunglasses for protection against the Mediterranean sun, as well as insect repellent if visiting during warmer months. Basic toiletries can be easily purchased in Genoa, but bring essentials such as toothbrush, toothpaste, and any specialized personal care items.

Travel Accessories

A lightweight backpack or daypack is handy for carrying essentials while exploring the city. Consider packing a reusable water bottle to stay hydrated throughout the day, especially in warmer weather. A small umbrella or raincoat is advisable as Genoa can experience occasional showers throughout the year.

Cultural and Practical Items

Pack a phrasebook or download a translation app to facilitate communication, as English may not be widely spoken in all areas. Bring a guidebook or map of Genoa to navigate the city and learn about its historical landmarks. If planning to visit churches or religious sites, respectful attire (covering shoulders and knees) is necessary.

Miscellaneous Items

Include a small first-aid kit with basic supplies such as bandages, pain relievers, and antiseptic wipes. If you enjoy journaling, consider bringing a notebook to record your travel experiences and impressions of Genoa. Don't forget to pack any specific items related to your interests, such as art supplies or a good book for leisurely moments.

5.4 Visa Requirements and Entry Procedures

Genoa, a captivating city on Italy's northwest coast, beckons visitors with its rich history, vibrant culture, and picturesque landscapes. Whether arriving by air, train, or road, understanding the visa requirements and entry procedures ensures a smooth and enjoyable journey.

By Air Travel

Travelers planning to reach Genoa by air typically land at Genoa Cristoforo Colombo Airport (GOA), conveniently located just 6 kilometers west of the city center. International visitors must ensure they have a valid passport with at least six months' validity beyond their intended stay. Italy is a member of the Schengen Agreement, which allows citizens from many countries to enter without a visa for up to 90 days within a 180-day period for tourism or business purposes. Upon arrival at Genoa Airport, passengers proceed through immigration control. Officials may request proof of sufficient funds for the duration of the stay, a return ticket, and accommodation details. It's advisable to carry printed or electronic copies of hotel reservations, travel itineraries, and contact information.

By Train

Traveling to Genoa by train offers scenic views and convenience, especially for visitors exploring other parts of Italy or arriving from nearby countries. Genoa's main train station, Genova Piazza Principe, is a major hub connecting the city with Milan, Turin, Rome, and other Italian cities, as well as international destinations via connecting services. Passengers arriving by train are subject to immigration procedures upon entering Italy. EU citizens can travel freely within Schengen countries using a national ID card or passport. Non-EU citizens should ensure they possess a valid Schengen visa if required. Immigration officials may ask for travel documents, including proof of accommodation and financial means.

By Road

Traveling to Genoa by road offers flexibility and the opportunity to explore the Italian countryside en route. Visitors arriving by car from within the Schengen Area should carry their national ID card or passport. Those from non-Schengen countries must possess a valid Schengen visa, allowing entry into Italy for tourism or business purposes. At border crossings, customs and immigration checks may be conducted. Officials may request proof of accommodation, a return ticket, and sufficient funds for the stay. It's essential to have vehicle registration documents, insurance, and an international driving permit if required.

General Entry Tips

Regardless of the mode of entry, visitors should prepare by familiarizing themselves with Italian customs regulations, which include restrictions on certain goods like alcohol and tobacco. It's advisable to carry essential medications in their original packaging and a prescription if necessary. For a seamless travel experience, staying informed about local regulations, cultural norms, and emergency contact numbers can be invaluable. Genoa welcomes visitors with open arms, offering a blend of historical landmarks, delectable cuisine, and Mediterranean charm that promises an unforgettable stay.

5.5 Safety Tips and Emergency Contacts

When embarking on a journey to Genoa, a city steeped in history and bustling with modern life, ensuring your safety and preparedness is paramount. Genoa, like any metropolitan area, presents both opportunities for exploration and potential challenges, making it essential to be informed and proactive throughout your visit.

Understanding Local Safety Dynamics

Genoa is generally a safe city for travelers, but as with any urban environment, it's wise to remain vigilant, especially in crowded tourist areas and on public transportation. Petty crime such as pickpocketing can occur, particularly in busy places like markets, train stations, and popular attractions. To mitigate risks, always keep your belongings secure, avoid displaying valuables openly, and use a money belt or secure bag.

Navigating Public Transportation Safely

Public transportation in Genoa, including buses and the metro, is efficient and commonly used by locals and tourists alike. While generally safe, it's advisable to be cautious during peak times and avoid isolated or poorly lit stations late at night. Keep an eye on your belongings and be aware of your surroundings when traveling on public transit.

Emergency Contacts

In case of emergencies, knowing whom to contact is crucial. The European emergency number, 112, works throughout Italy and connects you to police, fire, and medical services. For non-emergency police assistance or to report incidents, dial 113. Familiarize yourself with the nearest hospital or medical clinic to your accommodation, and keep their contact information handy.

Health and Medical Considerations

Ensure you have adequate health insurance coverage for your trip to Genoa. EU citizens can use their European Health Insurance Card (EHIC), but non-EU travelers should have comprehensive travel insurance that covers medical expenses abroad. Carry any necessary medications in their original containers, with a copy of your prescription if required.

Cultural Sensitivity and Local Customs

Respect for local customs and cultural norms is essential in Genoa. Italians appreciate polite behavior and modest dress, especially when visiting churches or religious sites. Keep in mind that public displays of affection are more reserved compared to some other countries. Understanding and respecting these cultural nuances will enhance your experience and interactions with locals.

Natural and Environmental Awareness

Genoa's natural beauty, including its coastline and parks, invites exploration. Whether hiking in the nearby mountains or strolling along the Ligurian Sea, be mindful of local environmental regulations and safety guidelines. Stay on marked trails, avoid disturbing wildlife, and carry out any trash you generate to help preserve these natural spaces for future visitors.

Communicating Effectively

While English is widely spoken in tourist areas and hotels, learning a few basic phrases in Italian can greatly enhance your experience and interaction with locals. Italians appreciate visitors who attempt to speak their language, even if it's just a few greetings and pleasantries.

Weather and Seasonal Considerations

Genoa experiences a Mediterranean climate, with hot summers and mild winters. Check the weather forecast before your trip and pack accordingly. Summers can be very hot and humid, while winters are mild but rainy. Umbrellas or raincoats are useful during the wetter months.

5.6 Currency Exchange and Banking Services

When planning a visit to Genoa, Italy, it's essential to understand the local currency, banking facilities, budgeting tips, and other financial matters that may affect your travel experience.

Currency Exchange and Banking Facilities

Genoa, like the rest of Italy, uses the Euro (€) as its official currency. Euros come in both coins and banknotes, with denominations ranging from €5 to €500. It's advisable to exchange your currency to Euros before arriving in Genoa for better rates. However, if you need to exchange money locally, there are numerous banks and exchange bureaus throughout the city.

Major Banks in Genoa

Several major banks operate in Genoa, offering a range of services suitable for visitors. UniCredit Italia, Intesa Sanpaolo, Banca Carige, Banco BPM, and Banca Mediolanum are among the prominent banking institutions. These banks provide services such as currency exchange, ATM facilities, international wire transfers, and multi-currency accounts.

Special Services for Visitors

UniCredit Italia- Located centrally, UniCredit offers multilingual services and assistance for foreign visitors, making it convenient for handling financial transactions.

Intesa Sanpaolo- Known for its extensive branch network, Intesa Sanpaolo provides specialized services such as travel insurance and tailored financial advice for tourists.

Banca Carige- With branches across Genoa, Banca Carige focuses on personalized customer service, including assistance in multiple languages and competitive exchange rates.

Banco BPM- Offers comprehensive banking services including currency exchange and investment advice, catering to both personal and business banking needs.

Banca Mediolanum- Known for innovative banking solutions, Banca Mediolanum provides digital banking options and personalized financial planning services.

Budgeting Tips

Genoa offers a range of budgeting options for travelers, from affordable accommodations and dining to luxury experiences. To manage expenses effectively, consider using credit cards widely accepted in Italy, such as Visa and MasterCard, while also carrying some cash for smaller establishments that may not accept cards.

Currency Exchange Bureaus

For visitors needing to exchange currency, several reputable exchange bureaus operate in Genoa. Locations near major tourist attractions and transport hubs include Piazza de Ferrari and Via XX Settembre, ensuring accessibility and competitive rates for exchanging your currency to Euros.

5.7 Language, Communication and Useful Phrases

Genoa, located in the Liguria region of Italy, is a city where Italian is predominantly spoken. While many locals, especially those working in tourism and hospitality sectors, understand and speak basic English, it is advisable to familiarize yourself with some Italian phrases to enhance your experience and interactions.

Useful Phrases for Visitors

Learning a few key phrases in Italian can greatly enrich your experience in Genoa:

-Greetings and Politeness: Start conversations with "Buongiorno" (Good morning) or "Buonasera" (Good evening). "Grazie" (Thank you) and "Prego" (You're welcome) are essential for expressing gratitude.

-Basic Communication: "Parla inglese?" (Do you speak English?) can be useful to inquire about someone's language proficiency. If needed, you can say "Non parlo italiano" (I don't speak Italian) to indicate your limitations.

-Ordering Food: When dining, phrases like "Posso avere il menu, per favore?"
(Can I have the menu, please?) and "Vorrei ordinare..." (I would like to order...)
are helpful. "Il conto, per favore" (The bill, please) is useful when concluding
your meal.

Communication Tips

In Genoa, as in much of Italy, locals appreciate efforts made to speak their language. Even if your Italian skills are basic, attempting to communicate in Italian often elicits a positive response. Many restaurants and shops in tourist areas have menus and signs in multiple languages, but smaller establishments may primarily use Italian.

Language Challenges and Solutions

While Italian is predominant, Genoa has a distinctive local dialect called Genoese (Genovese), which is derived from Ligurian. Though less commonly spoken today, some older residents may use it in informal settings. However, for practical purposes, standard Italian suffices for most interactions in the city.

Additional Tips for Language Navigation

-Phrasebooks and Apps: Carrying a small Italian phrasebook or using language translation apps can be invaluable for overcoming language barriers.
-Cultural Sensitivity: Italians value polite interactions, so phrases such as "Mi scusi" (Excuse me) and "Per favore" (Please) are appreciated.
-Learning Local Names: Familiarize yourself with local names for places and attractions. For example, the Old Town in Genoa is known as "Centro Storico" or simply "Il Centro."

Embracing Cultural Exchange

Visiting Genoa presents a wonderful opportunity to immerse yourself in Italian culture. Engaging with locals in their native language not only facilitates smoother interactions but also enriches your travel experience by fostering genuine connections and deeper understanding of the local way of life. In essence, while English can be a bridge language in tourist areas, embracing Italian phrases and customs enhances your journey through Genoa. It shows respect for the local culture and opens doors to authentic experiences that go beyond the surface of traditional tourist activities. Whether ordering a meal, exploring historic sites, or shopping in local markets, a basic understanding of Italian phrases will undoubtedly enhance your stay in this captivating Italian city.

5.8 Shopping and Souvenirs

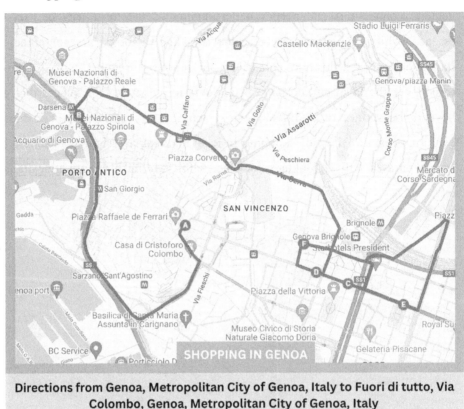

Directions from Genoa, Metropolitan City of Genoa, Italy to Fuori di tutto, Via Colombo, Genoa, Metropolitan City of Genoa, Italy

A
Genoa, Metropolitan City of Genoa, Italy

D
Palazzo delle Cupole, Via XX Settembre, Genoa, Metropolitan City of Genoa, Italy

B
Käsekaden, Via del Campo, Genoa, Metropolitan City of Genoa, Italy

E
Shopping street, Corso Buenos Aires, Genoa, Metropolitan City of Genoa, Italy

C
Éric, Piazza della Vittoria, Genoa, Metropolitan City of Genoa, Italy

F
Fuori di tutto, Via Colombo, Genoa Metropolitan City of Genoa, Italy

Genoa offers a diverse array of shopping experiences, from boutique stores to antique shops, each contributing to the city's vibrant retail scene. Whether you're looking for unique souvenirs, fashionable clothing, or locally crafted goods, Genoa's shopping districts cater to various tastes and preferences, ensuring a fulfilling shopping excursion.

Flumara

Flumara, located in the heart of Genoa's historic center, is renowned for its exquisite jewelry and accessories. This boutique showcases handcrafted pieces using precious metals and gemstones, reflecting both traditional Italian craftsmanship and contemporary design trends. Prices vary depending on the materials and intricacy of the pieces, catering to both luxury seekers and those looking for elegant souvenirs. Flumara is typically open from Monday to Saturday, with specific hours varying, so it's advisable to check in advance.

Kasekaden

For fashion enthusiasts, Kasekaden stands out as a destination for upscale clothing and accessories. Located in a chic area of Genoa, Kasekaden offers a curated selection of Italian and international designer brands, blending classic styles with modern trends. Visitors can explore a range of garments from casual wear to formal attire, with prices reflecting the quality and exclusivity of the items. The store operates daily, providing ample opportunity for shopping during both weekdays and weekends.

Eric

Eric is a concept store located near the waterfront, known for its eclectic mix of fashion, home decor, and lifestyle products. This boutique appeals to those seeking unique and artistic items, including locally sourced ceramics, textiles, and contemporary art pieces. Prices at Eric vary widely depending on the item's craftsmanship and materials, making it suitable for both budget-conscious shoppers and collectors looking to invest in distinctive pieces. The store is open throughout the week, making it convenient for spontaneous shopping excursions.

Palazzo delle Cupole

Palazzo delle Cupole, situated in a historic building in Genoa, is a haven for antique enthusiasts and collectors. This antique store specializes in furniture, artwork, and decorative objects spanning various periods and styles, offering a glimpse into Italy's rich cultural heritage. Prices at Palazzo delle Cupole can range significantly depending on the rarity and condition of the items, appealing to serious collectors and casual browsers alike. The store typically opens in the afternoon, aligning with the relaxed pace of Genoa's historical quarter.

Shopping Streets and Galleries

Genoa boasts several prominent shopping streets and galleries, such as Galleria Giuseppe Mazzini and Caruggi di Genova. Galleria Giuseppe Mazzini is a bustling arcade lined with boutiques, cafes, and specialty shops, ideal for fashion shopping and enjoying a leisurely stroll. Caruggi di Genova, the narrow alleyways of the old town, offer a treasure trove of artisanal products, including handmade leather goods, ceramics, and local delicacies. These areas are accessible on foot and are best explored during the daytime when shops are open and the atmosphere is lively.

Piazzi Luccoli and Fuori di Tutto

Piazzi Luccoli is a charming square known for its vibrant outdoor markets, where vendors sell everything from fresh produce to handmade crafts and antiques. This lively marketplace provides a glimpse into Genoa's local culture and is perfect for finding affordable souvenirs and gifts. Fuori di Tutto, on the other hand, is a quirky store specializing in vintage and retro items, from vinyl records to mid-century furniture and collectibles. Prices at these venues vary widely, offering opportunities for budget-friendly shopping and unique finds.

5.9 Health and Wellness Centers

Genoa offers a variety of health and wellness centers catering to different needs, whether you seek relaxation, rejuvenation, or specialized treatments. These centers provide an opportunity to unwind and take care of your well-being amidst the vibrant atmosphere of this historic city.

Spa and Wellness at Grand Hotel Savoia

Located in the heart of Genoa, the Grand Hotel Savoia offers a luxurious spa and wellness center that blends modern amenities with traditional Italian charm. Here, visitors can indulge in a range of treatments including massages, facials, and body therapies designed to promote relaxation and rejuvenation. The serene ambiance and professional staff ensure a pampering experience, making it an ideal retreat after a day of sightseeing.

Thalassotherapy at La Superba Spa

For those seeking therapeutic benefits from seawater, La Superba Spa provides thalassotherapy treatments overlooking the beautiful Ligurian Sea. Thalassotherapy utilizes seawater, seaweed, and marine mud to detoxify and revitalize the body. The spa offers a variety of baths, wraps, and massages tailored to improve circulation, relieve muscle tension, and promote overall wellness. The panoramic views of the Mediterranean enhance the calming effect of these treatments.

Ayurvedic Wellness at Shanti Ayurvedic Center

Experience the ancient healing traditions of India at Shanti Ayurvedic Center in Genoa. Specializing in Ayurveda, a holistic system of medicine, this center offers personalized consultations with experienced Ayurvedic practitioners who assess your constitution (dosha) and provide tailored treatments such as Abhyanga (oil massage), Shirodhara (oil pouring therapy), and Panchakarma (detoxification). These therapies aim to restore balance and harmony to the body and mind, promoting holistic wellness.

Yoga and Meditation at Centro Yoga Genova

Centro Yoga Genova provides a serene oasis in the bustling city, offering a variety of yoga classes suitable for all levels of experience. Whether you're a beginner or seasoned practitioner, you can participate in Hatha, Vinyasa, or Yin yoga sessions that focus on breathwork, alignment, and relaxation techniques. The center also hosts meditation workshops and retreats aimed at cultivating mindfulness and inner peace amidst the urban landscape of Genoa.

Fitness and Wellness at Virgin Active Genova

For those prioritizing fitness alongside relaxation, Virgin Active Genova offers state-of-the-art gym facilities, group exercise classes, and personalized training programs. Located conveniently within the city, this fitness center caters to diverse fitness goals with cardio machines, weight training equipment, and group classes such as yoga, Pilates, and cycling. After a workout, visitors can unwind in the sauna or steam room, ensuring a well-rounded approach to health and wellness.

5.10 Useful Websites, Mobile Apps and Online Resources

Planning a trip to Genoa involves more than just booking flights and accommodation. With the help of various websites, mobile apps, and online resources, visitors can enhance their travel experience by accessing essential information, navigating the city efficiently, and discovering hidden gems.

Visit Genoa Official Website: The Visit Genoa official website serves as a comprehensive guide for travelers, offering insights into the city's attractions, events, dining options, and practical information such as transportation and accommodation. It provides detailed descriptions of landmarks like the Palazzi dei Rolli and the Aquarium of Genoa, along with tips on exploring the historic center and nearby areas. The website is updated regularly with current events and seasonal activities, ensuring visitors stay informed throughout their stay.

Google Maps: Google Maps is indispensable for navigating Genoa's streets, whether on foot, by public transport, or driving. It provides real-time traffic updates, public transit schedules, and walking directions to landmarks and attractions. Offline maps are available for use without internet connectivity, making it reliable for exploring areas with potentially spotty reception. Visitors can also use the "Explore" feature to find nearby restaurants, cafes, and points of interest based on reviews and ratings.

Yelp: Yelp is a valuable resource for finding local businesses, restaurants, and services in Genoa. It offers user-generated reviews and ratings, helping visitors discover authentic dining experiences, cafes with WiFi, or specialty shops. The app allows filtering by price range, cuisine type, and opening hours, making it easier to plan meals and outings according to personal preferences. Additionally, Yelp provides insights into local culture through community feedback and recommendations.

Genova City Tour

The Genova City Tour app offers guided tours and audio guides for exploring Genoa's historical sites, cultural landmarks, and neighborhoods. It provides curated itineraries with detailed descriptions and historical context, enhancing the visitor's understanding of the city's rich heritage. The app includes interactive maps, multimedia content, and GPS navigation to ensure an immersive and informative tour experience. Users can choose from themed tours focusing on art, architecture, maritime history, and more.

Trenitalia and Moovit

For travelers using public transportation in Genoa, apps like Trenitalia and Moovit are essential tools. Trenitalia provides schedules, ticket booking options, and updates on train services connecting Genoa with other cities in Italy and Europe. Moovit offers real-time information on buses, trams, and metro services within Genoa, including route maps, service alerts, and estimated arrival times. Both apps help visitors navigate the city efficiently and plan their journeys using public transit.

5.11 Internet Access and Connectivity

Genoa offers several options for internet access, ensuring that travelers can stay connected, navigate the city, and access information effortlessly during their stay.

Wi-Fi Hotspots: Genoa provides numerous Wi-Fi hotspots throughout the city, particularly in tourist areas, hotels, cafes, and public spaces like parks and squares. Many restaurants and bars also offer free Wi-Fi to patrons. This allows visitors to check emails, use social media, and access maps without using mobile data.

SIM Cards and Mobile Data: For those preferring continuous connectivity, purchasing a local SIM card is a convenient option. Telecom Italia (TIM), Vodafone, and Wind Tre are major providers offering various prepaid SIM card options. These can be purchased at convenience stores, newsstands, and mobile carrier shops across the city. SIM cards typically include data plans that allow internet access on smartphones and tablets.

Mobile Apps for Travelers

Several mobile apps are particularly useful for travelers exploring Genoa:

Google Maps: Google Maps provides detailed maps, directions, and real-time traffic updates in Genoa. It's invaluable for navigating the city by foot, car, or public transportation.

WhatsApp: Beyond its messaging function, WhatsApp allows users to make voice and video calls over Wi-Fi or mobile data, making it ideal for staying in touch with friends, family, and local contacts.

Duolingo: For visitors interested in learning basic Italian or improving language skills, Duolingo offers free language lessons that can be completed offline after initial download.

MyTaxi: This app facilitates booking taxis in Genoa, providing fare estimates, driver ratings, and the ability to track your taxi's location in real-time.

XE Currency: XE Currency offers currency conversion rates and a calculator to help visitors understand local prices and manage expenses in their preferred currency.

Special Services of Mobile Apps

Google Maps stands out for its offline maps feature, allowing users to download maps of Genoa in advance and navigate without internet access. WhatsApp's ability to make calls over Wi-Fi is beneficial for international travelers looking to avoid roaming charges. Duolingo's offline mode allows users to continue learning Italian without requiring an internet connection, making it useful for downtime or travel periods without coverage. MyTaxi ensures efficient transportation around Genoa with options to pay via the app and track taxi arrivals in real-time, enhancing convenience and reliability. XE Currency is particularly helpful for travelers managing budgets and expenses, providing accurate exchange rates for informed spending decisions.

5.12 Visitor Centers and Tourist Assistance

When visiting Genoa, ensuring you have access to reliable tourist assistance and visitor centers can greatly enhance your experience. These centers provide valuable information, maps, guided tours, and other services to help you navigate and explore the city with ease.

Genoa Tourist Information Office: Located in the heart of the city at Via Garibaldi 12, the Genoa Tourist Information Office serves as a central hub for visitors. Here, you can obtain detailed maps, brochures, and information on attractions, events, and accommodations in Genoa and the surrounding areas. The staff are multilingual and knowledgeable, ready to assist with itinerary planning, transportation inquiries, and recommendations for dining and entertainment.

Porto Antico Tourist Information Center: Situated within the Porto Antico area, near the Aquarium of Genoa, this tourist information center caters specifically to visitors exploring the waterfront and its attractions. It offers specialized guidance on activities such as boat tours, visits to the Galata Maritime Museum, and access to the panoramic elevator at Bigo.

Genoa Cristoforo Colombo Airport Tourist Information: For those arriving by air, the tourist information desk at Genoa Cristoforo Colombo Airport provides essential services upon arrival. Located in the arrivals hall, the desk offers maps, transportation options to the city center, and assistance in booking accommodations. It's a convenient first stop to gather information and start your journey smoothly.

Genoa Railway Station Tourist Information Office: Travelers arriving by train will find the tourist information office at Genoa's main railway station, Genova Piazza Principe, invaluable. Staff here provide information on local transport connections, nearby attractions, and can assist with ticket purchases and reservations for tours or activities in and around Genoa.

Multilingual Assistance and Special Service: In addition to providing information, Genoa's visitor centers offer multilingual assistance in English, Italian, and often other major languages to accommodate international visitors. They can assist with booking guided tours, making restaurant reservations, and providing accessibility information for travelers with special needs.

Customized Tourist Assistance: For those seeking personalized assistance, many visitor centers in Genoa offer customized services such as guided tours tailored to specific interests like art, history, or food. These tours are often led by knowledgeable guides who can offer insights into Genoa's rich cultural heritage and hidden gems that might not be readily accessible without local expertise.

Emergency Support and Contact Information
It's reassuring to know that visitor centers also provide emergency support information, including contacts for local police, medical services, and embassy assistance if needed. They can advise on safety precautions, local regulations, and how to navigate any unexpected situations during your stay in Genoa.

CHAPTER 6
CULINARY DELIGHTS

6.1 Traditional Genoese Cuisine: Pesto, Focaccia, and Farinata

Traditional Genoese cuisine embodies the essence of Mediterranean flavors, offering a delightful array of dishes that reflect both local ingredients and historical influences. Among the highlights are Pesto, Focaccia, Farinata, and a few others that capture the essence of this vibrant coastal city.

Pesto alla Genovese

Undoubtedly the most famous culinary export from Genoa is Pesto alla Genovese, a vibrant green sauce bursting with the flavors of fresh basil, pine nuts, garlic, Parmesan cheese, and extra virgin olive oil. This aromatic sauce is traditionally pounded using a mortar and pestle to achieve the perfect consistency. Pesto is best enjoyed tossed with trofie or trenette pasta, allowing the pasta to absorb the sauce's rich flavors. Visitors to Genoa can savor authentic

Pesto alla Genovese at trattorias and osterias throughout the city, with prices typically ranging from €10 to €15 for a dish.

Focaccia Genovese

Another beloved Genoese staple is Focaccia Genovese, a soft and airy flatbread that showcases the region's exceptional olive oil. Lightly seasoned with sea salt and sometimes topped with rosemary or olives, Focaccia Genovese is a versatile snack enjoyed at any time of day. Locals often buy freshly baked focaccia from neighborhood bakeries, where it's sold by weight, costing around €3 to €5 for a generous portion. For visitors, a visit to a local bakery in the morning ensures the freshest experience, with the aroma of freshly baked bread filling the air.

Farinata

Farinata, also known as Cecina, is a savory pancake made from chickpea flour, water, olive oil, and salt. This simple yet flavorful dish has ancient origins and is baked until golden and crispy on the edges. In Genoa, Farinata is often enjoyed as a snack or appetizer, served hot and cut into slices. It's widely available in bakeries and food stalls across the city, typically costing around €2 to €4 per serving. For a truly authentic experience, visitors should look for places where Farinata is baked in a traditional wood-fired oven, ensuring a deliciously crisp texture.

Cappon Magro

Cappon Magro is a luxurious seafood salad that originated as a celebratory dish in Genoa during the 19th century. It features layers of seafood such as shrimp, lobster, and squid, arranged with vegetables and dressed with a rich green sauce made from parsley, capers, and anchovies. This elaborate dish is a testament to Genoa's maritime heritage and is often found in upscale restaurants along the coast, priced around €20 to €30 per portion. Visitors should consider trying

Cappon Magro as a main course or shared appetizer, paired with a crisp Ligurian white wine to complement its flavors.

Torta Pasqualina

For a taste of Genoa's traditional pies, Torta Pasqualina is a must-try. This savory pie is filled with a mixture of ricotta cheese, spinach, and often with the addition of eggs, all encased in layers of thin pastry. Torta Pasqualina is enjoyed year-round but holds particular significance during Easter celebrations. It can be found in bakeries and pastry shops across Genoa, priced between €8 to €12 depending on size and ingredients. Visitors can enjoy Torta Pasqualina warm or at room temperature, making it a convenient and delicious option for a picnic or light meal.

6.2 Seafood Specialties

Genoa stands as a vibrant hub where history, culture, and culinary excellence converge. Renowned for its maritime heritage and bustling port, the city offers a tantalizing array of seafood specialties that reflect its rich coastal bounty and culinary traditions. Here, visitors can embark on a gastronomic journey that showcases the freshest catches of the Mediterranean, prepared with skill and passion that are characteristic of Genoese cuisine.

Frittura di Pesce

One of the quintessential seafood delights of Genoa is the Frittura di Pesce, a delightful medley of lightly battered and fried fish and seafood. Typically, this dish includes tender calamari, succulent shrimp, and a variety of small fish such as anchovies or sardines, all fried to crispy perfection. Served hot and crispy, accompanied by a wedge of lemon and perhaps a sprinkle of sea salt, it embodies the simplicity and freshness that Genoa is celebrated for. You can savor this dish at traditional trattorias and seafood restaurants throughout the city, particularly around the historic Porto Antico area. Prices can vary, but expect to pay around €15-20 per person for a generous serving. For the best experience, opt for establishments recommended by locals or those with a long-standing reputation for quality seafood.

Pasta al Pesto con Gamberi

Another highlight of Genoese seafood cuisine is Pasta al Pesto con Gamberi, a dish that marries the region's famous basil pesto sauce with plump, juicy shrimp. The pesto, made from fresh basil leaves, pine nuts, garlic, Parmesan cheese, and extra virgin olive oil, is a vibrant green sauce that coats the pasta and shrimp with its aromatic flavors. This dish is a testament to Genoa's close connection to its agricultural hinterland and the Mediterranean Sea. You can enjoy Pasta al Pesto con Gamberi at trattorias and osterias scattered across the city, with prices typically ranging from €12-18 per serving. For an authentic experience, pair it with a crisp Ligurian white wine, such as Vermentino or Pigato.

Acciughe al Verde

Acciughe al Verde, or anchovies in green sauce, exemplifies Genoa's mastery in transforming humble ingredients into culinary delights. Fresh anchovies are marinated in a tangy green sauce made from parsley, garlic, vinegar, and olive oil, resulting in a dish that is both savory and refreshing. This preparation highlights the importance of preserving and enhancing the natural flavors of seafood without overpowering them. You can find Acciughe al Verde served as antipasto in traditional trattorias and seafood restaurants throughout Genoa. Prices vary depending on the establishment, but expect to pay around €8-12 for a plate. This dish pairs wonderfully with a glass of local sparkling wine or a chilled glass of Ligurian rosé.

Baccalà alla Genovese

Baccalà alla Genovese, or Genoese-style salted cod, is a dish that speaks to Genoa's historical maritime connections and its ability to preserve seafood for long sea voyages. Salted cod is rehydrated and then stewed in a rich tomato sauce with onions, olives, capers, and pine nuts, resulting in a robust and flavorful dish. The combination of sweet tomatoes, briny olives, and the delicate texture of the cod creates a harmonious flavor profile that is uniquely Genoese. You can enjoy Baccalà alla Genovese at traditional trattorias and osterias across the city, particularly in the historic district of the city center. Prices typically range from €15-25 per serving, depending on the portion size and restaurant ambiance.

Zuppa di Pesce

Zuppa di Pesce, or fish soup, is a hearty and soul-warming dish that showcases the depth of Genoa's seafood offerings. This flavorful soup is typically made with a variety of fish and shellfish, cooked slowly in a fragrant broth of tomatoes, garlic, olive oil, and aromatic herbs. The result is a dish that is both comforting and satisfying, perfect for cooler evenings along the Ligurian coast. Zuppa di Pesce is a staple in many seafood restaurants and trattorias in Genoa, especially those with a focus on traditional Ligurian cuisine. Prices can range from €18-25 per bowl, depending on the selection and freshness of seafood used. For the best experience, pair it with a slice of crusty Genoese focaccia and a glass of local white wine, such as Cinque Terre or Colli di Luni Vermentino.

6.3 Street Food: Best Markets and Food Stalls

Genoa not only charms visitors with its maritime history and stunning architecture but also tantalizes their taste buds with its vibrant street food scene.

Exploring Genoa's streets unveils a delightful array of culinary treasures that reflect the city's rich cultural heritage and love for authentic flavors. From bustling markets to hidden alleyway stalls, here's a journey through five iconic street foods that capture the essence of Genoa.

Focaccia Genovese

One cannot embark on a culinary exploration of Genoa without indulging in its renowned focaccia. This fluffy, olive oil-infused bread is a staple that locals and tourists alike savor throughout the day. The best place to experience the true essence of Focaccia Genovese is at the historic Mercato Orientale. Located in the heart of the city, this bustling market offers a variety of focaccia options, from classic topped with sea salt to variations with rosemary or olives. Prices generally range from €2 to €5 depending on the size and toppings. For the freshest experience, visit in the morning when batches emerge warm from the ovens.

Pesto alla Genovese

In Genoa, pesto isn't just a sauce; it's a culinary heritage. Made from fresh basil, pine nuts, Parmesan cheese, garlic, and olive oil, Pesto alla Genovese is a symphony of flavors that packs a punch. The best way to sample this iconic sauce is at the Mercato del Carmine. Here, tucked amidst colorful stalls, you'll find small eateries serving pasta dishes drenched in freshly made pesto. Prices for a pesto pasta plate typically range from €6 to €10. For a genuine experience, opt for handmade pasta and watch as skilled chefs whip up this Genoese delicacy before your eyes.

Farinata

A rustic yet beloved street food of Genoa, farinata is a savory pancake made from chickpea flour, olive oil, water, and salt. Locals enjoy it hot out of the oven, often paired with a sprinkle of black pepper. For the best farinata experience, head to Antica Sciamadda in the old town district. This historic eatery has been perfecting its farinata recipe for decades, offering a crispy yet creamy texture that melts in your mouth. Prices are around €3 to €4 per slice. Visit during lunch hours to savor it fresh from the oven, as locals do.

Acciughe al Verde

A testament to Genoa's love affair with the sea, acciughe al verde are green-hued anchovies marinated in a sauce made from parsley, garlic, vinegar, and olive oil. To taste this unique delicacy, make your way to the Mercato di Sant'Antonio. Here, amidst the vibrant market atmosphere, you'll find stalls offering fresh acciughe al verde served as antipasti or in a sandwich with local bread. Prices typically range from €5 to €8 per serving. Pair it with a glass of local wine for a true taste of Genoa's culinary heritage.

Panissa

For a taste of Genoa's rustic street food, panissa is a must-try. Originating from peasant cuisine, panissa is a fried fritter made from chickpea flour, water, and salt, often served in paper cones for a portable snack. Head to the Vucciria market near Piazza de Ferrari to find vendors offering freshly fried panissa. Prices are budget-friendly, usually around €2 to €3 per serving. Enjoy it as a quick bite while exploring the city's vibrant streets or as a late-night snack after a day of sightseeing.

6.4 Wine and Local Beverages

Genoa not only boasts a rich culinary tradition but also offers a diverse selection of local beverages that reflect the region's cultural and historical significance. From crisp white wines to unique liqueurs, the drinks of Genoa invite visitors to savor the essence of this vibrant coastal city.

Ligurian Wines

Genoa and its surrounding region of Liguria are renowned for producing distinctive wines that perfectly complement the local cuisine. Among the most notable are Vermentino and Pigato, both crisp and aromatic white wines that thrive in the region's coastal climate. These wines are often enjoyed alongside seafood dishes, enhancing the flavors with their citrusy notes and minerality. Visitors can find Ligurian wines in enotecas (wine bars), restaurants, and local markets throughout Genoa. Prices vary depending on the vintage and establishment, with a glass typically costing between €5 to €10, while bottles range from €15 to €30 or more for special selections.

Chinotto

Chinotto is a uniquely Genoese beverage made from the bitter fruit of the myrtle-leaved orange tree. It is cherished for its refreshing and slightly bitter taste, often likened to a cross between cola and citrus. Chinotto can be enjoyed on its own as a non-alcoholic soda or used as a mixer in cocktails. Bottled Chinotto is widely available in supermarkets and convenience stores across Genoa, with prices ranging from €1 to €3 per bottle. For visitors seeking a taste of local tradition, trying Chinotto paired with a slice of Focaccia Genovese is a delightful way to experience Genoa's flavors.

Sciacchetrà

Sciacchetrà is a rare and prized dessert wine that originates from the terraced vineyards of the Cinque Terre, a UNESCO World Heritage site near Genoa. Made from sun-dried grapes (typically Bosco, Albarola, and Vermentino varieties), Sciacchetrà is sweet and aromatic, with notes of honey, dried fruits, and spices. This amber-colored nectar is often served with biscotti or alongside desserts like Panettone during festive occasions. Visitors can find Sciacchetrà in select wine shops and upscale restaurants in Genoa, priced around €30 to €50 per bottle, reflecting its artisanal production and regional exclusivity.

Limoncello

While Limoncello is traditionally associated with Southern Italy, variations of this lemon liqueur can also be found in Genoa and the wider Ligurian region. Made from the zest of locally grown lemons steeped in alcohol and sweetened with sugar, Limoncello offers a zesty and refreshing digestif. It is commonly served chilled in small glasses after meals to aid digestion. Visitors can purchase bottles of Limoncello from liquor stores and specialty shops in Genoa, with prices typically ranging from €15 to €25 per bottle. Sampling Limoncello provides a delightful end to a meal, capturing the essence of Mediterranean citrus.

Basilico

Basilico is a traditional herbal liqueur from Genoa, crafted by infusing fresh basil leaves with alcohol and sugar. This aromatic liqueur boasts a vibrant green hue and a distinctly herbal flavor, reminiscent of the basil used in Pesto alla Genovese. Basilico is often enjoyed as a digestif, served chilled in small glasses. Visitors can find Basilico in local liquor stores and specialty shops around Genoa, priced approximately €20 to €30 per bottle. Sipping Basilico offers a unique taste of Genoa's culinary heritage, encapsulating the essence of fresh herbs and artisanal craftsmanship.

6.5 Top Restaurants and Dining Experiences

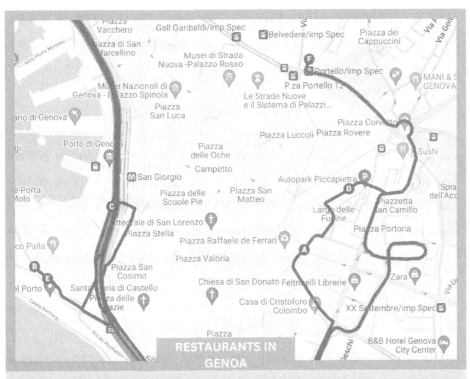

Directions from Genoa, Metropolitan City of Genoa, Italy to Le Rune, Adiacente a, Piazza del Portello, Genoa, Metropolitan City of Genoa, Italy

A

Genoa, Metropolitan City of Genoa, Italy

D

Trattoria da Maria, Vico Testadoro, Genoa, Metropolitan City of Genoa, Italy

B

Osteria di Vico Palla, Vico Palla, Genoa, Metropolitan City of Genoa, Italy

E

Piazza Cavour, 21, Genoa, Metropolitan City of Genoa, Italy

C

Il Marin, Calata Cattaneo, Genoa, Metropolitan City of Genoa, Italy

F

Le Rune, Adiacente a, Piazza del Portello, Genoa, Metropolitan City of Genoa, Italy

Genoa boasts a culinary scene that blends traditional Italian flavors with innovative techniques, offering visitors a tantalizing array of dining experiences. From cozy trattorias serving homemade pasta to upscale restaurants showcasing Ligurian seafood delicacies, the city caters to every palate with its diverse gastronomic offerings.

Antica Osteria di Vico Palla: Located in the heart of Genoa's historic center, Antica Osteria di Vico Palla is a revered institution known for its authentic Ligurian cuisine. This charming osteria dates back to the 17th century and retains its rustic ambiance with stone walls and wooden beams. The menu features specialties such as Pansoti filled with walnut sauce, and Trofie al Pesto, showcasing the region's famed basil sauce. Local wines like Vermentino and Pigato complement the dishes perfectly. Prices are moderate, with pasta dishes starting around €12 and main courses averaging €20. Antica Osteria di Vico Palla is open for lunch from 12:00 PM to 3:00 PM and for dinner from 7:00 PM to 10:30 PM, making it an ideal spot for both leisurely lunches and intimate dinners.

Il Marin: Perched on the waterfront in Porto Antico, Il Marin offers diners breathtaking views of the harbor alongside a menu focused on fresh seafood. Specialties include Spaghetti allo Scoglio (seafood pasta) and Frittura di Paranza (mixed fried fish), sourced directly from the Ligurian Sea. The restaurant's elegant interior features maritime-themed decor, creating a sophisticated yet relaxed atmosphere. Prices at Il Marin reflect its waterfront location, with pasta dishes starting around €15 and seafood mains averaging €25 to €30. Open daily from 12:00 PM to 3:00 PM for lunch and from 7:00 PM to 11:00 PM for dinner, Il Marin is a popular choice for both locals and tourists seeking a taste of Genoa's maritime heritage.

Trattoria da Maria: Tucked away in the vibrant district of Carignano, Trattoria da Maria is a family-run gem celebrated for its homestyle Genoese dishes. The trattoria exudes a cozy ambiance with checkered tablecloths and walls adorned with vintage photographs. Signature dishes include Stoccafisso alla Genovese (salted cod in tomato sauce) and Pansoti with walnut sauce. Local wines and homemade desserts like Torta della Nonna (Grandmother's cake) complete the dining experience. Prices are affordable, with pasta dishes starting at €10 and main courses ranging from €15 to €20. Trattoria da Maria is open for lunch from 12:00 PM to 2:30 PM and for dinner from 7:00 PM to 10:30 PM, offering visitors a taste of traditional Genoese hospitality.

Cavour 21: Situated in the elegant Piazza Cavour, Cavour 21 is a modern trattoria known for its inventive twists on classic Ligurian recipes. The restaurant's sleek interior features contemporary decor and large windows overlooking the bustling square. The menu showcases dishes like Ravioli di Zucca e Gamberi (pumpkin and shrimp ravioli) and Tagliata di Tonno (tuna steak). A carefully curated wine list highlights regional labels alongside Italian favorites. Prices at Cavour 21 are moderate to upscale, with pasta dishes starting around €15 and main courses averaging €25 to €30. Open daily from 12:30 PM to 3:00 PM for lunch and from 7:30 PM to 11:00 PM for dinner, Cavour 21 offers a sophisticated dining experience in the heart of Genoa.

Le Rune: Le Rune offers diners a picturesque setting with views of the quaint fishing village and the Ligurian Sea. This seafood-focused restaurant prides itself on using locally sourced ingredients to create dishes such as Risotto allo Scampi (langoustine risotto) and Moscardini alla Ligure (baby octopus Ligurian style). The interior is cozy with maritime-themed decor, perfect for a romantic dinner or a relaxed lunch by the sea. Prices at Le Rune reflect its quality and location, with pasta dishes starting at €18 and seafood mains averaging €30 to €35. The restaurant is open daily from 12:00 PM to 3:00 PM for lunch and from 7:00 PM to 11:00 PM for dinner, providing visitors with a memorable dining experience amidst the charm of Boccadasse.

CHAPTER 7
DAY TRIPS AND EXCURSIONS

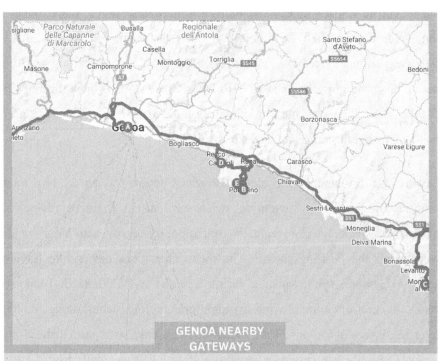

GENOA NEARBY
GATEWAYS

Directions from Genoa, Metropolitan City of Genoa, Italy to Savona, Province of Savona, Italy

A
Genoa, Metropolitan City of
Genoa, Italy

D
Camogli, Metropolitan City of Genoa,
Italy

B
Portofino, Metropolitan City of
Genoa, Italy

E
San Fruttuoso abbey, Via S. Fruttuoso,
Camogli, Metropolitan City of Genoa,
Italy

C
Cinque Terre, SP, Italy

F
Savona, Province of Savona, Italy

7.1 Portofino and the Italian Riviera

Genoa serves as an ideal gateway to explore the stunning Italian Riviera, a region renowned for its picturesque landscapes, charming villages, and azure Mediterranean waters. Day trips from Genoa offer a delightful blend of history, natural beauty, and culinary delights, making them perfect for travelers seeking a mix of relaxation and exploration.

Portofino

Located a mere 35 kilometers southeast of Genoa lies the exclusive seaside village of Portofino, often referred to as the jewel of the Italian Riviera. Accessible by various modes of transportation including train, bus, or even by boat, Portofino captivates visitors with its pastel-colored houses, upscale boutiques, and tranquil harbor dotted with luxury yachts. The journey from Genoa typically takes around one hour by train, offering scenic views of the coastline along the way. Once in Portofino, visitors can explore the historic Castello Brown perched on a hilltop, providing panoramic views of the village and the Ligurian Sea. Stroll along the waterfront promenade lined with cafes and restaurants, where fresh seafood dishes and local wines await. Nature enthusiasts can embark on hikes through the Regional Natural Park of Portofino, known for its Mediterranean flora and fauna, or relax on the pebbled beaches that dot the coastline.

Santa Margherita Ligure and Rapallo

For a day of seaside elegance and relaxation, consider visiting Santa Margherita Ligure and Rapallo, two neighboring towns located approximately 30 kilometers southeast of Genoa. Accessible by train or bus with a travel time of around 45 minutes, these towns exude a laid-back charm with palm-lined promenades, elegant villas, and scenic harbors filled with fishing boats and pleasure yachts. In Santa Margherita Ligure, visitors can explore the 16th-century Basilica of Santa Margherita d'Antiochia, relax on the sandy beaches, or stroll through the gardens of Villa Durazzo, a historic estate overlooking the sea. Rapallo, known for its medieval castle and picturesque waterfront, offers opportunities for boat trips to nearby attractions such as the Abbey of San Fruttuoso or simply enjoying a leisurely seafood lunch with views of the Gulf of Tigullio.

Chiavari and Sestri Levante

For a quieter and less touristy experience, consider exploring Chiavari and Sestri Levante, two charming towns located approximately 40-50 kilometers southeast of Genoa. Accessible by train with travel times ranging from 30 minutes to one hour, Chiavari and Sestri Levante offer a blend of historic architecture, pristine beaches, and local charm.

Logistics and Costs

Transportation costs from Genoa to these destinations vary depending on the mode of travel and season. Trains are generally reliable and affordable, with tickets ranging from €5 to €15 for a one-way journey, depending on the destination. Buses and boats also provide alternative routes to some locations, offering flexibility for day trips.

7.2 Cinque Terre

Approximately 90 kilometers southeast of Genoa, Cinque Terre consists of five charming villages - Monterosso al Mare, Vernazza, Corniglia, Manarola, and Riomaggiore - each nestled in rugged coastal terrain overlooking the Ligurian Sea. The most convenient way to reach Cinque Terre from Genoa is by train, with frequent services departing from Genoa's main station, Genova Brignole. The journey takes around 1.5 to 2 hours, offering breathtaking views of the coastline along the way. Visitors to Cinque Terre can expect to explore narrow cobblestone streets, enjoy fresh seafood in local trattorias, and swim in crystal-clear waters. Each village has its own unique charm; Monterosso is known for its beaches, Vernazza for its picturesque harbor, and Manarola for its vineyards and stunning sunset views. Hiking enthusiasts can traverse the scenic Sentiero Azzurro trail, which connects all five villages and offers spectacular vistas of the rugged coastline.

Portofino

Another gem of the Ligurian coast, Portofino is a short distance from Genoa, approximately 35 kilometers southeast. Accessible by car or bus, the journey takes about 45 minutes to an hour. Portofino is famous for its upscale harbor lined with pastel-colored buildings, luxury yachts, and exclusive boutiques. Visitors can explore the historic Castello Brown, hike up to the Church of San

Giorgio for panoramic views, or relax at one of the waterfront cafes enjoying freshly caught seafood and local wines.

Santa Margherita Ligure

Located just south of Portofino, Santa Margherita Ligure is a charming seaside town known for its elegant villas, palm-fringed promenade, and vibrant local markets. The town is easily accessible from Genoa by train or bus, with a travel time of around 40 minutes to one hour. Visitors can stroll along the seafront, visit the 16th-century Basilica of Santa Margherita d'Antiochia, or take a boat tour to nearby resorts and hidden coves along the coast.

Genoa Nervi and Portovenere

Closer to Genoa, Nervi offers a peaceful escape with its historic parks, waterfront promenade, and the beautiful Anita Garibaldi Walk. It's a short train ride from Genoa's city center, providing a tranquil setting ideal for a leisurely day trip. Portovenere, on the other hand, located about 100 kilometers southeast of Genoa, can be reached by train followed by a short boat ride or by car in approximately 1.5 to 2 hours. This UNESCO World Heritage site features medieval architecture, a stunning seafront castle, and the famous Church of San Pietro perched on a rocky promontory.

7.3 Camogli and San Fruttuoso Abbey

Genoa serves as an ideal gateway to explore the picturesque gems of Camogli and the tranquil San Fruttuoso Abbey. Each destination offers a distinct blend of natural beauty, historical intrigue, and local charm, making them perfect day trips from the bustling port city.

Camogli: Just a short train ride or drive from Genoa, Camogli beckons with its colorful waterfront homes, inviting beaches, and authentic maritime atmosphere.

The journey from Genoa takes approximately 30 minutes by train, making it easily accessible for day-trippers seeking a serene coastal retreat. Upon arrival, visitors are greeted by the iconic sight of Camogli's pastel-hued buildings cascading down to the azure waters of the Ligurian Sea. Stroll along the waterfront promenade, where local fishermen still mend their nets against the backdrop of bobbing boats. Camogli's pebbled beach invites relaxation, whether you choose to sunbathe or dip into the refreshing Mediterranean waters. Don't miss the opportunity to sample freshly caught seafood at one of the charming trattorias lining the harbor, where the scent of anchovies frying in local olive oil permeates the air.

San Fruttuoso Abbey

A short boat ride from Camogli lies the secluded haven of San Fruttuoso Abbey, nestled within a small cove accessible only by sea or on foot. The journey by ferry from Camogli takes approximately 15 minutes, offering breathtaking views of the rugged coastline and emerald waters along the way. Stepping ashore, visitors are greeted by the tranquil ambiance of San Fruttuoso, where the abbey's ancient walls and serene cloisters tell tales of centuries past. Originally founded by Greek monks in the 10th century, the abbey later became a refuge for weary travelers and a place of spiritual contemplation.

Surrounded by lush Mediterranean vegetation and steep cliffs plunging into the sea, San Fruttuoso invites exploration of its hidden corners and secluded beach. The crystal-clear waters are ideal for snorkeling or simply soaking in the natural beauty of this remote sanctuary. A hike through the surrounding hills offers panoramic vistas of the Ligurian coastline, rewarding adventurers with sweeping views that stretch as far as Portofino in the distance.

Logistics and Costs

To embark on this journey, travelers can take a regional train from Genoa to Camogli, with tickets costing around €5-10 per person each way, depending on the class and time of booking. Boat trips from Camogli to San Fruttuoso Abbey typically cost between €10-15 round-trip, offering a scenic maritime experience that enhances the day's adventure.

7.4 The Ligurian Alps and Hiking Trails

Offering a stark contrast to the sun-drenched Mediterranean coast, this mountainous region provides an ideal retreat for outdoor enthusiasts and nature lovers alike. Day trips from Genoa to the Ligurian Alps promise breathtaking landscapes, serene hiking trails, and a glimpse into the rich natural and cultural heritage of northern Italy.

Monte Beigua

Approximately 40 kilometers northeast of Genoa, Monte Beigua Regional Park stands as a gateway to the Ligurian Alps. Accessible by car or public transportation with a travel time of around one hour, Monte Beigua offers a diverse terrain of rugged peaks, lush valleys, and ancient beech forests. Hiking enthusiasts can choose from a network of well-marked trails that cater to all skill levels, ranging from leisurely strolls to challenging ascents. Visitors can expect to encounter a variety of flora and fauna endemic to the region, including rare orchids, chamois, and eagles soaring overhead. Panoramic viewpoints such as Monte Grosso and Rocca della Penna offer sweeping vistas of the Ligurian coastline and the surrounding Alpine peaks, providing ample opportunities for photography and contemplation amidst nature's grandeur.

Aveto Natural Regional Park

Situated approximately 70 kilometers southeast of Genoa, Aveto Natural Regional Park beckons with its tranquil alpine meadows, crystal-clear streams, and towering peaks. Accessible by car in about 1.5 to 2 hours, this lesser-known gem offers a pristine wilderness experience away from the hustle and bustle of city life. Hikers can explore trails that wind through dense forests of beech, chestnut, and fir, leading to hidden waterfalls such as the Cascata del Lavacchiello. The park is also home to diverse wildlife, including roe deer, wild boar, and foxes, making it a haven for nature enthusiasts and photographers alike. During the summer months, the park's high-altitude pastures burst into bloom with vibrant wildflowers, creating a spectacle of color against the backdrop of rugged peaks.

Val Trebbia

Venturing northeast from Genoa, approximately 50 kilometers away, lies Val Trebbia, often referred to as the "Valley of Castles" due to its picturesque medieval fortresses and ancient villages. Accessible by car or bus with a travel time of around one to two hours, Val Trebbia offers a blend of natural beauty and historical charm. Visitors can explore the hilltop village of Bobbio, home to the impressive Ponte Gobbo (Hunchback Bridge) spanning the Trebbia River, or wander through the cobbled streets of Ottone and Marsaglia, where time seems to stand still. Hiking trails meander through chestnut groves and vineyards, leading to panoramic viewpoints such as Monte Penice, offering sweeping vistas of the valley below and the Ligurian Apennines in the distance.

Alta Via dei Monti Liguri

For seasoned hikers seeking a more challenging adventure, the Alta Via dei Monti Liguri (High Way of Ligurian Mountains) presents an epic trekking experience traversing the entire length of the Ligurian Alps. Spanning approximately 440 kilometers from Ventimiglia to Ceparana, this long-distance trail showcases the region's diverse landscapes, from coastal cliffs to alpine meadows. Sections of the Alta Via can be accessed from various points near Genoa, with popular starting points including Colle di Cadibona and Passo del Faiallo. Hikers can expect steep ascents, rugged terrain, and remote mountain refuges offering basic accommodations and meals. Highlights along the trail include panoramic ridgelines, ancient stone villages, and encounters with local shepherds tending their flocks amidst the solitude of the mountains.

Val Fontanabuona

Southwest of Genoa, approximately 40 kilometers away, Val Fontanabuona invites visitors to explore its rich cultural heritage and scenic hiking trails. Accessible by car or bus with a travel time of around one hour, this valley is dotted with charming villages known for their traditional stone houses and artisanal crafts. Hikers can embark on trails that wind through chestnut forests and olive groves, passing by ancient chapels and rural hamlets where time-honored traditions still thrive. The village of Varese Ligure, with its well-preserved medieval architecture and bustling piazza, serves as a gateway to the surrounding hillsides offering panoramic views of the valley below.

Logistics and Costs

Transportation costs from Genoa to the Ligurian Alps vary depending on the chosen destination and mode of travel. Rental cars provide flexibility for exploring remote areas, while public buses and regional trains offer affordable options for accessing trailheads and starting points. Entrance fees to regional parks and nature reserves are generally nominal or free, encouraging visitors to immerse themselves in the natural beauty and cultural richness of the Ligurian Alps.

7.5 Savona and Its Beaches

Savona is conveniently located approximately 50 kilometers west of Genoa, making it easily accessible by both train and car. The train journey from Genoa to Savona typically takes around 30 to 45 minutes, with frequent services departing from Genova Brignole or Genova Piazza Principe stations. Traveling by car along the A10 highway offers a picturesque drive of about one hour, showcasing scenic views of the Ligurian coastline.

Savona

Upon arrival in Savona, visitors are greeted by a city rich in maritime heritage and medieval charm. The historic city center, with its well-preserved architecture and winding streets, invites exploration on foot. Highlights include the imposing Priamar Fortress, overlooking the sea and housing museums that delve into Savona's naval history and art.

Savona's Beaches

Savona boasts several beautiful beaches that cater to all tastes, whether seeking family-friendly shores or secluded spots for quiet relaxation. The main beach, Bagni Lido, offers amenities such as sun loungers, umbrellas, and beachfront cafes, making it a popular choice for both locals and tourists. Those looking for a more natural setting can visit the pristine beach of Bagni Al Mare, known for its crystal-clear waters and scenic surroundings.

Cost of Transportation and Activities

The cost of transportation from Genoa to Savona varies depending on the mode of travel. Train tickets typically range from €5 to €15 per person for a one-way journey, while fuel costs for a car trip may average around €10 to €15 each way. Entrance fees to attractions like the Priamar Fortress are modest, ensuring that exploring Savona remains affordable for visitors.

Cultural Delights

In addition to its coastal allure, Savona offers cultural delights that enrich the day trip experience. The Cappella Sistina di Savona, a stunning chapel adorned with intricate frescoes, and the Cathedral of Santa Maria Assunta with its impressive Gothic architecture are must-see landmarks for history enthusiasts. Visitors can also wander through the lively markets, sampling local delicacies such as focaccia and fresh seafood.

Local Cuisine and Dining

No visit to Savona is complete without indulging in its delectable cuisine. Seafood lovers can savor dishes like risotto ai frutti di mare (seafood risotto) or trofie al pesto di zucchine e gamberi (trofie pasta with zucchini pesto and shrimp). The city's vibrant dining scene offers options ranging from cozy trattorias serving traditional Ligurian fare to elegant restaurants overlooking the harbor.

CHAPTER 8

ENTERTAINMENT AND NIGHTLIFE

8.1 Theatres and Opera Houses

Genoa beckons travelers with its rich cultural tapestry and vibrant arts scene, particularly evident in its diverse array of theatres and opera houses. Each venue offers a unique glimpse into the city's historical and artistic legacy, promising unforgettable experiences for visitors.

Teatro Carlo Felice; stands as a majestic testament to Genoa's enduring love affair with opera. Located in the heart of the city, this grand opera house has been meticulously restored to its 19th-century glory, boasting a stunning neo-classical façade and an opulent interior adorned with intricate frescoes and gilt details. The Teatro Carlo Felice hosts world-class opera performances and ballets throughout the year, drawing aficionados and newcomers alike with its impeccable acoustics and emotive storytelling. Tickets can vary depending on the production, but experiencing a performance here is not merely a show; it's an immersion into the soul-stirring passion of Italian opera.

Teatro della Corte; offers a more intimate setting for theatrical performances, tucked away in Genoa's atmospheric historic center. This charming theatre embraces a more experimental approach, showcasing contemporary plays, musicals, and even intimate concerts. What sets Teatro della Corte apart is its dedication to fostering emerging talent and pushing artistic boundaries, making it a hotspot for those seeking avant-garde performances that challenge and inspire. Tickets are generally affordable, making it accessible for both locals and tourists eager to explore Genoa's modern cultural pulse.

Palazzo Ducale; transcends the traditional notion of a theatre, serving as a multifaceted cultural hub where art, music, and theatre converge. Once the seat of power for the Doges of Genoa, this sprawling palace now hosts a diverse array of cultural events, from art exhibitions to theatre productions and classical concerts. Its labyrinthine corridors and majestic courtyards provide a breathtaking backdrop for cultural immersion, inviting visitors to wander through centuries of history while enjoying world-class performances. The ticket prices vary depending on the event, offering something for every taste and budget.

Teatro Stabile di Genova; epitomizes the city's commitment to preserving and celebrating its theatrical heritage. Founded in the 1940s, this renowned theatre company has nurtured generations of talented actors and directors, staging both classical masterpieces and contemporary works that resonate with modern audiences. Located in the vibrant district of Castelletto, Teatro Stabile di Genova offers a rich program that includes everything from Shakespearean dramas to cutting-edge productions by emerging playwrights. The theatre's inclusive atmosphere and reasonable ticket prices make it a favorite among locals and tourists seeking authentic cultural experiences.

Teatro della Tosse; exudes a bohemian charm that captivates visitors from the moment they step inside. Housed in a former church, this unconventional theatre celebrates artistic experimentation and cultural diversity through its eclectic repertoire of performances. From experimental theatre and contemporary dance to multimedia art installations, Teatro della Tosse challenges conventions and sparks conversations about pressing social issues. Ticket prices are typically affordable, reflecting its commitment to making the arts accessible to all.

8.2 Live Music Venues and Concert Halls

Genoa, a city steeped in maritime history and rich cultural heritage, offers a vibrant music scene that resonates through its diverse live music venues and concert halls. Nestled amidst the ancient streets and bustling piazzas are hidden gems where melodies weave through the air, enticing both locals and travelers alike to immerse themselves in the rhythm of the city.

Teatro Carlo Felice; a grand opera house located in the heart of Genoa, stands as a beacon of classical music and theatrical performances. Established in the 19th century and rebuilt after World War II, it boasts a striking neoclassical façade and a majestic interior adorned with plush velvet seats and ornate balconies. The venue hosts a range of performances from opera to symphony concerts, drawing music enthusiasts to indulge in its timeless elegance. Ticket prices vary depending on the event and seating, offering something for both seasoned patrons and curious newcomers.

La Claque; emerges as a cozy haven for those seeking intimate live music experiences. Tucked away in the atmospheric district of Carignano, this eclectic venue exudes a bohemian charm with its mismatched furniture and candlelit ambiance. From jazz ensembles to acoustic sets, La Claque curates a calendar of performances that captivate audiences with their raw authenticity and soulful expression. The entry fees are modest, reflecting its commitment to fostering a community of music lovers who appreciate the allure of lesser-known talents.

Palazzo Ducale; not just a historical landmark but also a cultural hub, transforms its courtyard into a mesmerizing open-air stage during the summer months. Located in the heart of the city's historic center, this Renaissance palace resonates with echoes of the past while embracing contemporary arts and music. Visitors can savor alfresco concerts under the starlit sky, where the backdrop of ancient architecture merges with the melodic strains of diverse musical genres.

Lanterna del Mare; perched at the edge of the sea, offers a unique fusion of music and maritime charm. This iconic lighthouse-turned-cultural space hosts seasonal concerts that celebrate Genoa's maritime legacy through music. Whether it's the rhythmic beats of Mediterranean folk music or the haunting melodies of sea shanties, Lanterna del Mare transports audiences on a sensory journey across the waves. The admission fees are typically nominal, allowing visitors to indulge in an evening of music while soaking in panoramic views of the Ligurian Sea, creating a truly unforgettable experience.

Casa della Musica; Genoa's contemporary music scene with a dynamic lineup of concerts and events. This modern cultural center serves as a platform for emerging artists and established performers alike, showcasing genres ranging from indie rock to experimental electronic music. With its state-of-the-art acoustics and versatile spaces, Casa della Musica fosters an immersive audiovisual experience that resonates with the city's youthful energy and creative spirit. Ticket prices vary depending on the event, offering accessibility without compromising on the quality of the musical offerings.

8.3 Bars and Pubs: Historical and Modern Spots

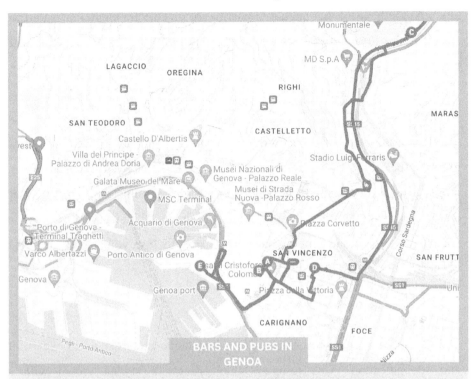

BARS AND PUBS IN GENOA

Directions from Genoa, Metropolitan City of Genoa, Italy to Bar Berto, Piazza delle Erbe, Genoa, Metropolitan City of Genoa, Italy

A	D
Genoa, Metropolitan City of Genoa, Italy	Alchimia, Via San Vincenzo, Genoa, Metropolitan City of Genoa, Italy

B	E
La Claque in Agorà, Vico di San Donato, Genoa, Metropolitan City of Genoa, Italy	Osteria di Vico Palla, Vico Palla, Genoa, Metropolitan City of Genoa, Italy

C	F
The Ghost Club, Via Piacenza, Genoa, Metropolitan City of Genoa, Italy	Bar Berto, Piazza delle Erbe. Genoa, Metropolitan City of Genoa: Italy

Genoa pulsates with a vibrant nightlife that captivates both locals and visitors alike. At the heart of this nocturnal energy are its eclectic nightclubs and dance floors, each offering a distinct experience that promises to immerse you in the city's rich cultural tapestry.

Azimut Club

Located in the heart of the historic city center, Azimut Club beckons with its pulsating beats and lively atmosphere. Step into this sleek venue where DJs spin a mix of international hits and local favorites, creating an electrifying ambiance that keeps the dance floor alive until the early hours. With its modern decor and friendly vibe, Azimut Club is the perfect spot to lose yourself in music and connect with Genoa's nightlife scene.

La Claque

Tucked away in a chic corner of the city, La Claque exudes an air of exclusivity and sophistication. This intimate club attracts a stylish crowd with its avant-garde interiors and curated selection of music, ranging from deep house to jazz-infused rhythms. Sip on expertly crafted cocktails at the bar or mingle in the cozy lounge areas, where conversation flows as smoothly as the beats. La Claque promises a night of elegance and refinement, making it a must-visit for those seeking a taste of Genoa's upscale nightlife.

Ghost Club

Step through the doors of Ghost Club and journey back in time to the roaring twenties. Housed in a meticulously restored historical building, this club combines old-world charm with contemporary flair. The sprawling dance floor invites you to dance under the glow of ornate chandeliers, while live performances and themed nights add to the mystique of the experience. Whether you're a history buff or simply in search of a unique night out, Ghost Club promises an unforgettable evening steeped in nostalgia and allure.

Lighthouse Cafe

Lighthouse Cafe offers a magical setting overlooking the shimmering waters of the Ligurian Sea. Located on Genoa's picturesque waterfront, this open-air venue transforms into a dance paradise after sunset. Groove to eclectic beats played by local DJs, surrounded by the gentle sea breeze and the sparkling lights of passing ships. Lighthouse Cafe is not just a nightclub; it's a serene escape where music meets nature, creating a truly enchanting atmosphere.

Alchimia

In the vibrant district of Carignano, Alchimia stands out as a hub of creativity and diversity. This artsy nightclub embraces a bohemian spirit, attracting a diverse crowd of artists, musicians, and free spirits. The eclectic playlist spans genres from techno to indie, ensuring there's something for every musical taste. The interior decor, adorned with quirky artworks and vintage furniture, sets the stage for a laid-back yet lively evening. Alchimia is where Genoa's avant-garde community comes together to dance, converse, and celebrate the city's cultural richness.

8.4 Nightclubs and Dance Floors

Genoa, with its labyrinthine alleys and bustling piazzas, offers a delightful mix of historical charm and modern vibrancy when it comes to its bars and pubs. Whether you're seeking a cozy spot steeped in centuries-old history or a trendy hangout pulsating with contemporary energy, the city caters to every taste and mood, promising unforgettable evenings immersed in local flavors and conviviality.

Antica Osteria di Vico Palla

Antica Osteria di Vico Palla stands out as a hidden gem tucked away in the historic heart of Genoa. Dating back to the 16th century, this osteria exudes old-world charm with its vaulted ceilings, rustic wooden furniture, and warm candlelit ambiance. Patrons can savor traditional Ligurian dishes paired with an extensive selection of local wines and artisanal liqueurs. Prices here are reasonable, offering excellent value for authentic Italian hospitality amidst a setting that feels frozen in time.

La Casa del Burro

La Casa del Burro offers a whimsical twist on Genoa's pub scene, located in the eclectic district of Carignano. Translating to "The House of the Donkey," this quirky establishment combines a cozy pub atmosphere with a penchant for craft beers and inventive cocktails. The decor is eclectic, featuring mismatched furniture, vintage posters, and a lively crowd that spills onto the outdoor terrace during warmer months. Prices for drinks are mid-range, making it a popular haunt for both locals and visitors looking to unwind in a laid-back yet spirited setting.

Ferrovia Genova Bar

Ferrovia Genova Bar pays homage to Genoa's industrial heritage, located near the city's main train station. This stylish bar channels a sleek, minimalist vibe with its exposed brick walls, contemporary furnishings, and soft lighting that creates an inviting ambiance after a day of exploring. The menu showcases a fusion of classic Italian aperitivos and innovative mixology, accompanied by a selection of gourmet bar bites. While slightly higher in price, the experience promises sophistication and a taste of Genoa's evolving cocktail culture.

Bar Berto

Bar Berto epitomizes the quintessential Italian coffee bar experience, nestled in the vibrant district of San Fruttuoso. Since 1947, this family-run institution has been a beloved gathering spot for morning espressos, afternoon aperitivos, and late-night digestivos. The atmosphere is lively and convivial, with locals and tourists alike mingling at the marble-topped counters or spilling onto the outdoor terrace. Prices are affordable, making it ideal for sampling traditional Italian coffee alongside aperitivos like Aperol Spritz or Negroni.

L'Arturo

L'Arturo offers a contemporary twist on Genoa's traditional wine bars, located in the picturesque neighborhood of Castelletto. This modern enoteca boasts a curated selection of regional wines, complemented by a menu of gourmet small plates featuring local cheeses, cured meats, and freshly baked focaccia. The ambiance is sophisticated yet approachable, with sleek interior design and panoramic views of the city skyline. Prices for wines vary, catering to both casual wine enthusiasts and connoisseurs seeking new discoveries in Ligurian viticulture.

8.5 Annual Festivals and Cultural Events

Genoa, a city that pulsates with history and creativity, invites travelers to immerse themselves in its vibrant tapestry of annual festivals and cultural events. Throughout the year, these celebrations weave together the city's rich heritage, culinary delights, and artistic flair, offering a kaleidoscope of experiences that leave a lasting imprint on all who participate.

Genoa International Boat Show

Genoa International Boat Show is held every September at the iconic Fiera di Genova, stands as a testament to the city's maritime prowess. This prestigious event draws sailing enthusiasts and industry professionals from around the globe to marvel at the latest yacht designs, technological innovations, and marine accessories. Against the backdrop of Genoa's historic port, visitors can explore a dazzling array of luxury vessels and partake in workshops and demonstrations. The show's dynamic atmosphere and waterfront location make it a must-visit for anyone captivated by the allure of the sea.

Euroflora

Euroflora, a botanical extravaganza held biennially in Genoa's enchanting parks and gardens, blooms to life in April and May. This internationally acclaimed floral exhibition transforms the city into a breathtaking floral paradise, showcasing stunning displays of rare plants, vibrant blooms, and imaginative garden designs. Visitors can wander through themed pavilions, attend horticultural workshops, and witness floral artistry at its finest. Euroflora not only celebrates the beauty of nature but also fosters a sense of environmental stewardship, making it a captivating event for garden enthusiasts and nature lovers alike.

Genoa International Poetry Festival

Genoa International Poetry Festival takes center stage each June, enchanting audiences with the lyrical beauty of words. Held at various historic venues throughout the city, this literary celebration brings together poets, writers, and thinkers from diverse cultures and languages. Poetry readings, performances, and discussions create a dialogue that transcends borders, offering profound insights into the human experience. The festival's intimate settings and passionate recitations evoke a sense of shared humanity, making it a poignant cultural experience that resonates long after the final verse is spoken.

Genoa Science Festival

Genoa Science Festival, held annually in October, ignites curiosity and wonder through a series of interactive exhibitions, workshops, and lectures. Spanning across museums, universities, and public spaces, this interdisciplinary festival explores cutting-edge scientific research and technological advancements in engaging and accessible ways. From astronomy to robotics, visitors of all ages can delve into the mysteries of the universe, participate in hands-on experiments, and interact with leading scientists. The festival's emphasis on innovation and discovery fosters a spirit of inquiry and inspires the next generation of thinkers and inventors.

Genoa Film Festival

Genoa Film Festival, held in November, spotlights the art of cinema against the backdrop of the city's historic theaters and modern cinemas. This annual event showcases a diverse selection of international films, documentaries, and shorts, providing a platform for emerging filmmakers and established auteurs alike. Film screenings, Q&A sessions with directors, and special events create a dynamic atmosphere that celebrates cinematic storytelling in all its forms. The festival's program reflects Genoa's cinematic heritage and contemporary film culture, offering cinephiles and casual moviegoers alike an opportunity to explore new narratives and cinematic visions.

CONCLUSION AND INSIDER TIPS

As you conclude your journey through the pages of the *"Genoa Travel Guide 2024 and Beyond,"* you've embarked on a discovery of a city that pulsates with history, culture, and an irresistible allure. Genoa, with its winding medieval streets, panoramic views of the Ligurian Sea, and vibrant culinary scene, invites you to immerse yourself in its unique charm and uncover hidden gems around every corner.

Insider Tips for Your Genoa Adventure

Embrace the Aperitivo Culture: Join the locals in a cherished tradition of pre-dinner drinks and small bites. Head to the narrow streets of the old town to find quaint bars offering delicious local wines like Vermentino and refreshing Aperol Spritz. It's not just about the drinks but also the opportunity to mingle and soak in the lively atmosphere.

Explore Beyond the Famous Sites: While the Palazzi dei Rolli and the Aquarium are must-see attractions, venture further to discover lesser-known treasures. Wander through the atmospheric alleys of Boccadasse, a charming fishing village within the city, or hike up to Castello d'Albertis for breathtaking views over the cityscape and harbor.

Dine Like a Local: Genoa is a paradise for food enthusiasts. Don't miss the chance to savor traditional dishes such as pesto alla genovese, focaccia di Recco, and freshly caught seafood at local trattorias and osterias. Venture into Mercato Orientale for a sensory feast of fresh produce, regional cheeses, and artisanal delicacies.

Immerse Yourself in the Arts: Beyond its rich maritime history, Genoa boasts a thriving cultural scene. Visit Palazzo Ducale for contemporary art exhibitions, attend an opera performance at Teatro Carlo Felice, or explore the eclectic exhibitions at Museo di Palazzo Reale. Art and history converge seamlessly in this dynamic city.

Navigating the City: While Genoa's historic center is best explored on foot, utilize the efficient public transportation system for longer journeys. Consider purchasing a Genova Card for discounted access to museums, public transport, and guided tours, ensuring a seamless and budget-friendly exploration of the city.

As you plan your visit, embrace the insider tips that enhance your experience, allowing you to connect with Genoa on a deeper level and create memories that will last a lifetime. Let your curiosity guide you as you embark on an unforgettable journey through Genoa's storied past and dynamic present.

Made in the USA
Las Vegas, NV
05 January 2025

15849207R00077